NORTH CAROLINA
STATE BOARD OF COMMUNITY COLLEGES
LIBRARIES
SOUTHEASTERN COMMUNITY COLLEGE

SOUTHEASTERN
COLLEGE LIBRARY
WHITEVILLE, N. C. 28472

FAMOUS POEMS EXPLAINED

HELPS TO

READING WITH THE UNDERSTANDING

WITH BIOGRAPHICAL NOTES OF THE AUTHORS REPRESENTED

BY

WAITMAN BARBE, Litt. D.

ASSOCIATE PROFESSOR OF THE ENGLISH LANGUAGE AND LITERATURE,
WEST VIRGINIA UNIVERSITY

WITH AN INTRODUCTION BY

RICHARD G. BOONE, PH. D.

FORMERLY SUPERINTENDENT CINCINNATI PUBLIC SCHOOLS, AND PRESIDENT
MICHIGAN NORMAL COLLEGE

Granger Poetry Library

GRANGER BOOK CO., INC.
Great Neck, NY

First Published 1909
Reprinted 1979

INTERNATIONAL STANDARD BOOK NUMBER
0-89609-106-6

LIBRARY OF CONGRESS CATALOG NUMBER
78-73480

PRINTED IN THE UNITED STATES OF AMERICA

PREFACE

This book is intended as a hand-book for teachers and as a help for students. Its purpose is to aid in the comprehension and understanding, and therefore in the appreciation, of literature through the poems here presented.

With two or three exceptions, these poems are taken from various standard School Readers, and most of them are recognized as being among the great short poems of English and American literature. Not all of them, however, are found in any one set of Readers; and it is hoped that the book may be found suitable for use as a supplementary Reader with any of the standard series.

Literature classes in the common schools, high schools, and other secondary schools, are generally expected to give attention to many of these poems. Moreover, there is a large and increasing number of private students of literature all over the country whom the author has had in mind. He would like to be of some help to them.

In reading with the understanding two things are essential—a clear and full knowledge of the meaning of the piece read, and the vivid and definite use of the imagination on the part of the reader. This book aims to supply in some measure the means to the first requisite.

The arrangement is, in the main, the pedagogical one—the easier selections at the beginning, and the more difficult ones towards the end of the book.

Following the body of the book will be found biographical notes, in alphabetical order, of the authors represented, together with brief lists of their works most worthy to be read or studied.

My grateful acknowledgments are hereby made to my colleagues, Professors Robert Allen Armstrong and John Harrington Cox, of the Department of English, and Dr. James Morton Callahan, of the Department of History, for valuable assistance; and to Dr. Charles William Kent, Professor of English Literature in the University of Virginia, for looking over the manuscript.

W. B.

WEST VIRGINIA UNIVERSITY,
December 1, 1908.

CONTENTS.

TITLE	AUTHOR	PAGE
Introduction	Richard Gause Boone	7
The Charge of the Light Brigade	Alfred Tennyson	11
Hohenlinden	Thomas Campbell	15
The Gift of Empty Hands	Sarah M. B. Piatt	18
Bannockburn	Robert Burns	21
The Star-Spangled Banner	Francis Scott Key	23
To a Waterfowl	William Cullen Bryant	27
The Sandpiper	Celia Thaxter	31
The Reaper and the Flowers	Henry W. Longfellow	34
Down to Sleep	Helen Hunt Jackson	36
The Bluebell	Julia A. Eastman	38
Make Way for Liberty	James Montgomery	41
The Rising in 1776	Thomas Buchanan Read	46
The Singing Lesson	Jean Ingelow	51
Faithless Nelly Gray	Thomas Hood	55
Burial of Sir John Moore	Charles Wolfe	58
The Burial of Moses	Cecil Frances Alexander	61
The American Flag	Joseph Rodman Drake	65
Old Ironsides	Oliver Wendell Holmes	68
The Battle of Blenheim	Robert Southey	70
Columbus	Joaquin Miller	76
Chicago: October 10, 1871	Bret Harte	80
The Wreck of the Hesperus	Henry W. Longfellow	81
King Solomon and the Ants	John Greenleaf Whittier	87
The Destruction of Sennacherib	George Gordon Byron	91
Robin Hood	John Keats	96
The Night before Waterloo	George Gordon Byron	100

CONTENTS.

TITLE	AUTHOR	PAGE
The Chambered Nautilus	Oliver Wendell Holmes	105
Wolsey's Farewell to Cromwell	William Shakespeare	108
The Rainy Day	Henry Wadsworth Longfellow	113
In an Age of Fops and Toys	Ralph Waldo Emerson	115
O Captain! My Captain!	Walt Whitman	116
Aladdin	James Russell Lowell	119
The Old Clock on the Stairs	Henry W. Longfellow	122
The Four Winds	Charles Henry Luders	126
The Birds of Killingworth	Henry W. Longfellow	128
The Light of Other Days	Thomas Moore	141
The Isle of Long Ago	Benjamin Franklin Taylor	143
Recessional	Rudyard Kipling	146
The Ladder of St. Augustine	Henry W. Longfellow	149
Ichabod	John Greenleaf Whittier	153
The Bugle Song	Alfred Tennyson	156
Where Lies the Land?	Arthur Hugh Clough	158
The Rhodora	Ralph Waldo Emerson	159
The Finding of the Lyre	James Russell Lowell	161
The Sands o' Dee	Charles Kingsley	163
Abou ben Adhem	Leigh Hunt	165
Gillespie	Henry Newbolt	167
Excelsior	Henry Wadsworth Longfellow	170
The Isles of Greece	George Gordon Byron	174
On First Looking into Chapman's Homer	John Keats	180
Break, Break, Break	Alfred Tennyson	182
Tubal Cain	Charles Mackay	184
The Raven	Edgar Allan Poe	188
Armageddon	Edwin Arnold	198
Each and All	Ralph Waldo Emerson	203
Fate	Bret Harte	206
Fortune	Alfred Tennyson	208
Ulalume	Edgar Allan Poe	209
Prospice	Robert Browning	216
Crossing the Bar	Alfred Tennyson	218

INTRODUCTION

By "learning to read," as usually understood, is meant coming to know words and their surface meanings, and how to take the obvious import of simple sentences. But one may have passed into the higher classes, so called, and into the secondary school even, or beyond, and yet be unable to "read" with an understanding or with an enriching content. To read means more than to interpret isolated words, or sentences, or even groups of sentences. It means the ability to take meaning from the printed page—but articulate meaning, the meaning of the whole through thinking together the meanings of the parts. If the parts are not interpreted, or are misinterpreted, the interpretation of the whole suffers. Longfellow's *Rainy Day* has a meaning as a whole, distinct from but arising from the ideas and pictures of the several stanzas and lines composing it. The first stanza of that poem furnishes a fairly complete picture, as does the second; but the meaning of neither is the meaning of the poem. In the third are summed up or converged the threads of suggestion in the other two. But even this would be incomplete, ineffective, without its setting in the materials of the first and second. To read the *Rainy Day* implies getting this articulate meaning; finding, beholding the composite picture, seeing and enjoying each part in terms of the whole. Moreover, both the understanding and the appreciation of the whole is enhanced by the content of meaning and beauty one is able to find in the parts; the clearness with which the picture elements and ideas take their places in the finished product; the quality and amount of experience one is able to converge upon the assembled words.

To "read," therefore, implies, further, somewhat of the dramatic sense, an educated faculty for marshalling details and significant elements, and picturesque situations, and their maneuvering to a common end of meaning. And the integrity of the whole is imperiled by any defect in the understanding of the parts making up the whole. One may take the meanings of all the words and every line in *Rainy Day,* and yet fail of the picture of the whole; but *this* is inevitably wanting without *those* meanings. Their threads make up the warp of the completed fabric. The woof, or filling, must be furnished out of the riches of one's own experience and understanding. To "read," then, means the construction of mental pictures that shall be true to the materials used.

All this implies, further, an element of joy in both getting and enriching the content of the text; a sense of pleasure in the creative and interpreting act; finding pleasure in the picture given or made, being able to domesticate it among one's own experiences. This is the final test of all literature for each reader. It must make its appeal as something to be embraced, and fondled, and lived. It must touch the heart. But if it be made up of unfamiliar experiences, or alien ideas, transcendent ideals, or vague conceptions, the picture suffers. Only the understanding heart reads aright— the appreciative heart, the dramatic creative sense, reenforced by a rich experience, the discriminating mind that furnishes material for a discriminating appreciation.

Literature, as one of the Fine Arts, is the product, the cumulative product, of the race's effort to give expression to its highest ideals concerning human spirit, and the achievements of the soul. All growth in the literature sense means, whatever else is implied, the power and disposition to appropriate type images and ideals as permanent facts in one's experience; ideas and ideals in terms of which the conduct of life is expressed.

This little book is an intelligent and purposeful attempt to open the way for an easy access of some real ideals to the heart of the pupil. Specimens of what is believed to possess high literary merit only have been selected; specimens, too, of beautiful imagery and noble ideals; selections easily accessible to teachers, and all of them suited to public school use.

It would obviously be unwise to attempt an inventory of the race's ideals which such literature seeks to express; but some typical ones may be suggested as binding together the great literatures of which the selections in this book are examples.

Running through most of them is the conception of the ideal individual; sometimes the ideal family relation; the ideal civic relation; the ideal economic relation; and the ideal moral, cultural, and social relations. But, always and everywhere, real literature gives expression to one or another of such enduring ideals, in attractive form and with appealing force. It is a store of these that gives richness to mental life; and it is one function of purposeful education to put the child into intelligent, loving possession of them.

RICHARD G. BOONE.

FAMOUS POEMS EXPLAINED

THE CHARGE OF THE LIGHT BRIGADE

The famous charge of the English Light Brigade, immortalized in Tennyson's poem, took place at the battle of Balaklava, during the Crimean War, October 25, 1854. Balaklava is not far from Sebastopol on the borders of the Black Sea. The story is a thrilling one of bravery and of obedience to orders. The full strength of the Russian army, covered from attack by thirty guns, lay at a distance of a mile and a half from the armies of the allies (English, French, and Turks). Mackenzie's *The 19th Century* gives these particulars:

"Up to this time our Light Cavalry Brigade had not been engaged. Lord Lucan, their commander, now received by the hand of Captain Nolan a written order to advance nearer to the enemy. On reading this order Lord Lucan asked its bearer how far they were to advance. He received a reply which he construed, with fatal inaccuracy, to signify that it was his duty to charge the enemy. The Light Brigade made itself ready to attack the Russian army. Every man knew that some terrible mistake was sending the brigade to destruction, but no man shrunk from his duty of obedience. They rode straight down the valley towards the wondering Russians and in full view of the chiefs of their own army, powerless now to restrain them. As the excitement of battle gained power over men and horses the pace increased. The shot of the Russian guns tore through their ranks, but did not abate the speed of their advance, the fierceness of their attack. They galloped their horses between the Russian guns, cutting down the gunners as they passed. They rode down and scattered several squadrons of cavalry. And then they paused, and turned back, and galloped toward the shelter of British lines. The Russians reopened upon them with grape and canister. Their return was beset by an overwhelming force of Russian cavalry; but they cut their way through and reached the position they had left scarcely half an hour before. Six hundred and seventy men went forth to that memorable ride, but only one hundred and ninety-eight came back."

Murdock's *The Reconstruction of Europe* says that the brigade would have been utterly destroyed, wiped out of existence, but for the brilliant and timely charge of a French company which attracted the attention of the Russians away from the English, leaving the valley comparatively clear for a few minutes for the retreat of the remnant of the Light Brigade.

Compare with this the story of Arnold von Winkelried, page 41; and the story of Thermopylæ, in any history of Greece.

THE CHARGE OF THE LIGHT BRIGADE

1

Half a league, half a league,
 Half a league onward,
All in the valley of Death
 Rode the six hundred.
"Forward, the Light Brigade!
Charge for the guns!" he said:
Into the valley of Death
 Rode the six hundred.

2

"Forward, the Light Brigade!"
Was there a man dismayed?
Not tho' the soldier knew
 Some one had blundered:
Theirs not to make reply,
Theirs not to reason why,
Theirs but to do and die:
Into the valley of Death
 Rode the six hundred.

3

Cannon to right of them,
Cannon to left of them,
Cannon in front of them
 Volley'd and thunder'd;

Storm'd at with shot and shell,
Boldly they rode and well,
Into the jaws of Death,
Into the mouth of Hell
  Rode the six hundred.

4

Flash'd all their sabres bare,
Flash'd as they turned in air
Sabring the gunners there,
Charging an army, while
  All the world wonder'd;
Plunged in the battery-smoke
Right thro' the line they broke;
Cossack and Russian
Reel'd from the sabre-stroke
  Shatter'd and sunder'd.
Then they rode back, but not,
  Not the six hundred.

5

Cannon to right of them,
Cannon to left of them,
Cannon behind them
  Volley'd and thund'red;
Stormed at with shot and shell,
While horse and hero fell,
They that had fought so well
Came through the jaws of Death,

Back from the mouth of Hell,
All that was left of them,
  Left of six hundred.

6

When can their glory fade?
O the wild charge they made!
  All the world wondered.
Honor the charge they made!
Honor the Light Brigade,
  Noble six hundred!

—Lord Tennyson.

HOHENLINDEN

Hohenlinden means *tall lindens*. It is the name of a great dense and dark forest in Upper Bavaria. In an open space in the very midst of this great forest stands the village of Hohenlinden, nineteen miles east of Munich. The battle of Hohenlinden occurred December 3, 1800, during one of Napoleon's campaigns, between the French under Moreau and the Austrians under Archduke John. It was fought in a blinding snowstorm. The Austrians lost twenty thousand men and the French five thousand.

> Few, few shall part where many meet!
> The snow shall be their winding-sheet.

This is one of the best war poems in the language. It was in the late Charles A. Dana's famous list of "ten best poems." The poem should be read first as a whole, then studied line by line, and finally read again somewhat rapidly as a whole. It is a combination of stirring pictures artistically blended with thrilling effect—if the reader has the imagination to re-create the hills of stained snow, the waving banners, and all the dreadful revelry that Munich and Linden saw on that awful night.

HOHENLINDEN

1

On Linden, when the sun was low,
All bloodless lay the untrodden snow,
And dark as winter was the flow
    Of Iser, rolling rapidly.

2

But Linden saw another sight,
When the drum beat at dead of night,
Commanding fires of death to light
    The darkness of her scenery.

3

By torch and trumpet fast arrayed,
Each horseman drew his battle-blade,
And furious every charger neighed,
    To join the dreadful revelry.

HOHENLINDEN

4

Then shook the hills with thunder riven,
Then rushed the steed to battle driven,
And louder than the bolts of heaven
  Far flashed the red artillery.

5

But redder yet that light shall glow
On Linden's hills of stainèd snow,
And bloodier yet the torrent flow
  Of Iser, rolling rapidly.

6

'T is morn, but scarce yon level sun
Can pierce the war-clouds, rolling dun,
Where furious Frank and fiery Hun
  Shout in their sulphurous canopy.

7

The combat deepens. On, ye brave,
Who rush to glory, or the grave!
Wave, Munich! all thy banners wave,
  And charge with all thy chivalry!

8

Few, few shall part where many meet!
The snow shall be their winding-sheet;
And every turf beneath their feet
  Shall be a soldier's sepulcher.
                              —Thomas Campbell.

Linden is an abbreviated form of the name of the forest where the battle was fought. It is situated between the river Iser and the river Inn—

". . . dark as winter was the flow of Iser, rolling rapidly."

Frank—the French; *Hun*—the Austrians; *fires of death*—flashes of artillery.

Bloodier yet the torrent flow—The waters of the Iser are said to have been literally red with blood.

Sulphurous canopy—smoke of the guns.

War-clouds, rolling dun—smoke of battle.

Chivalry here has its primary meaning of cavalry, from *cheval*, a horse.

THE GIFT OF EMPTY HANDS

Once upon a time two young princes were condemned to death by a certain king. They pleaded for their lives, and each promised the king that if his life were spared he would bring rich and wonderful gifts to the king. The king consented and the two princes started out to seek for the gifts.

One of them had remarkably good luck; everything he sought he secured without the slightest effort or trouble. A rare bird lit on his arm, the most beautiful rose in the world fell on his breast, costly gems lay at his feet.

The other strove manfully to keep his promise, but in spite of all of his efforts he secured nothing. His hands were torn and his feet were bruised in his effort to keep his promise to the king, but fate was against him.

The two princes went back to the king at the time agreed upon, the one with his choice gifts, in obtaining which he had made no effort whatever, the other with empty but bleeding hands.

The king accepted the sincere but futile efforts of the one rather than the easily obtained gifts of the other.

THE GIFT OF EMPTY HANDS

1

They were two princes doomed to death;
Each loved his beauty and his breath:
"Leave us our life and we will bring
Fair gifts unto our lord, the king."

2

They went together. In the dew
A charmèd bird before them flew.
Through sun and thorn one followed it;
Upon the other's arm it lit.

3

A rose, whose faintest flush was worth
All buds that ever blew on earth,
One climbed the rocks to reach; ah, well,
Into the other's breast it fell.

4

Weird jewels, such as fairies wear,
When moons go out, to light their hair,

One tried to touch on ghostly ground;
Gems of quick fire the other found.

5

One with the dragon fought to gain
The enchanted fruit, and fought in vain;
The other breathed the garden's air
And gathered precious apples there.

6

Backward to the imperial gate
One took his fortune, one his fate:
One showed sweet gifts from sweetest lands,
The other, torn and empty hands.

7

At bird, and rose, and gem, and fruit,
The king was sad, the king was mute;
At last he slowly said: "My son,
True treasure is not lightly won.

8

"Your brother's hands, wherein you see
Only these scars, show more to me
Than if a kingdom's price I found
In place of each forgotten wound."
—Sarah M. B. Piatt.

True treasure is not lightly won—This is the true and beautiful lesson of *The Gift of Empty Hands*. It is the lesson that the Master taught over and over—not what we do, but what we try to do. Or, as Browning says in *Saul:* "'T is not what man does which exalts him, but what man would do."

BANNOCKBURN

The battle of Bannockburn was fought in 1314, near Stirling castle, in the Lowlands of Scotland, by the English forces under King Edward II. and the Scots in command of Robert Bruce. It resulted in a decisive victory for the Scots, and later in the recognition of Scotland as a kingdom independent of England. The struggle for Scottish independence had been going on for a long time; and notwithstanding the fact that one king of Scotland had been deposed and banished, and the crown and other emblems of royalty taken away to London, the Scottish people were not conquered. Under various leaders, particularly William Wallace, who came to be the great national hero, they carried on the struggle. Wallace was captured, taken to London, tried for treason, and executed, 1305. The legends of this bold and chivalrous outlaw are the treasures of Scottish story, poetry, and song. The next year after the execution of Wallace, Robert Bruce declared himself king of Scotland, and, calling all classes of Scotsmen around him for a last great struggle, won the splendid victory of Bannockburn.

This is the historical setting of Burns's famous poem, the best war-ode, Carlyle thought, "that was ever written by any pen."

The lines are supposed to be spoken by Bruce to his heralds on the morning of the battle. Of course this address is purely imaginary, but it is just such an address as the Scots who had with Wallace bled would receive with unspeakable enthusiasm.

Of the manner of the composition of the poem Carlyle says: "It was composed on horseback, in riding in the middle of tempests over the wildest Galloway moor, in company with a Mr. Syme. . . . Doubtless this stern hymn was singing itself, as he formed it, through the soul of Burns; but to the external ear it should be sung with the throat of the whirlwind."

BANNOCKBURN

1

Scots, wha hae wi' Wallace bled;
Scots, wham Bruce has often led;
Welcome to your gory bed,
    Or to victorie.

2

Now's the day, and now's the hour;
See the front o' battle lour;
See approach proud Edward's pow'r—
    Chains and slaverie!

3

Wha will be a traitor-knave?
Wha can fill a coward's grave?
Wha sae base as be a slave?
    Let him turn and flee!

4

Wha for Scotland's king and law
Freedom's sword will strongly draw,
Free-man stand, or free-man fa'?
    Let him follow me!

5

By oppression's woes and pains!
By your sons in servile chains!
We will drain our dearest veins,
    But they shall be free!

6

Lay the proud usurpers low!
Tyrants fall in every foe!
Liberty's in every blow!
    Let us do, or die!

—Robert Burns.

Jane Porter's stirring novel, *Scottish Chiefs,* published 1810, has for its heroes Robert Bruce and William Wallace.

THE STAR-SPANGLED BANNER

The flag that floated over Fort McHenry, the original *star-spangled banner,* now belongs to Mr. Eben Appleton, of New York. Recently it was lent to the Smithsonian Institution at Washington. It is an immense banner, twenty-eight by thirty feet, and shows the effects of battle and age.

FAMOUS POEMS EXPLAINED

More interest attaches to this stirring poem than ever before, since the United States army has recognized it as our national anthem. *General Orders No. 201* of the War Department, published December 15, 1906, contains the following regulation:

> Whenever *The Star-Spangled Banner* is played by the band on a formal occasion at a military station, or at any place where persons belonging to the military service are present in their official capacity, all officers and enlisted men present stand at attention, and if not in ranks render the prescribed salute, the position of the salute being retained until the last note of *The Star-Spangled Banner*. The same respect is observed toward the national air of any other country when it is played as a compliment to official representatives of such country. Whenever *The Star-Spangled Banner* is played as contemplated by this paragraph the air is played through once without the repetition of any part, except such repetition as is called for by the musical score.

The effect of this order is not confined to military circles, but it is the custom in many parts of the country for the audience to rise and for gentlemen to remove their hats whenever *The Star-Spangled Banner* is played. It is now very generally accepted as the American national air.

The poem was written by Francis Scott Key on Wednesday morning, September 14, 1814, when the British forces were attacking Baltimore (War of 1812). The flag referred to was flying over Fort McHenry. Key was temporarily a prisoner on the British flagship *Surprise* (later transferred to a cartel or ship for the

THE STAR-SPANGLED BANNER

exchange of prisoners), where he had gone to secure the release of his friend, Dr. Beanes, a prominent physician of Upper Marlborough, Maryland. Fort McHenry was bombarded all day Tuesday and Wednesday, and at the same time a land attack was being made on Baltimore. The land attack failed and the British decided that retreat was inevitable unless the fort were taken. At one o'clock Wednesday night a tremendous fire, at close range, was opened on Fort McHenry; five hundred bombs fell within the ramparts and many more burst over them. The firing was at such close quarters that dense smoke enveloped both fort and ships from midnight till morning. John C. Carpenter, in the *Century Magazine,* July, 1894, says: "The long hours were unbearable. Key had seen the fate of Washington and anticipated the fate of Baltimore. At seven the suspense was unrelaxed. The firing from the fleet ceased. The large ships loomed indistinct and silent in the mist. To the west lay the silent fort, the white vapor heavy upon it. With eager eye Key watched the distant shore, till in a rift over the fort he dimly discerned the flag still proudly defiant. In that supreme moment was written *The Star-Spangled Banner."*

The song was printed in broadsheet form in the office of the Baltimore *American,* the type being set by a boy of twelve, all the other printers having gone to the defense of the city. It was sung in all the camps around the city, and soon spread over the country. The tune is a vagrant air, familiar in many countries.

THE STAR-SPANGLED BANNER

1

O say, can you see, by the dawn's early light,
  What so proudly we hailed at the twilight's last
    gleaming—
Whose broad stripes and bright stars, through the perilous fight,
  O'er the ramparts we watched were so gallantly
    streaming!
And the rocket's red glare, the bombs bursting in air,
Gave proof through the night that our flag was still
    there;
O say, does that star-spangled banner yet wave
O'er the land of the free and the home of the brave?

2

On that shore dimly seen through the mist of the deep,
  Where the foe's haughty host in dread silence reposes,
What is that which the breeze, o'er the towering steep,
  As it fitfully blows, now conceals, now discloses?
Now it catches the gleam of the morning's first beam,
In full glory reflected now shines on the stream;
'T is the star-spangled banner; O long may it wave,
O'er the land of the free and the home of the brave!

*   *   *   *   *   *   *

4

O thus be it ever, when freemen shall stand
  Between their loved homes and the war's desolation!

Blest with victory and peace, may the heav'n-rescued
 land
  Praise the power that hath made and preserved us a
  nation.
Then conquer we must, when our cause it is just,
And this be our motto,—"In God is our trust":
And the star-spangled banner in triumph shall wave
O'er the land of the free and the home of the brave.
                              —Francis Scott Key.

Read Drake's *The American Flag* in this volume and Ryan's *The Conquered Banner.*

TO A WATER-FOWL

On December 15, 1815, William Cullen Bryant walked from his home at Cummington, Mass., to Plainfield, Mass., to begin the practice of the law. He was 21 years of age—the age when every thoughtful young man's mind is an interrogation point, the age when he is asking a thousand questions which cannot be answered. Bryant had spent two years at Williams College and had planned to continue his studies at Yale, but was not financially able to do so. He wanted to be a poet, and had already written *Thanatopsis* (with the exception of the last paragraph, which was not written until he was twenty-eight), but he knew that he could not make a living out of poetry; he wanted to be an editor, but there were few editorial openings those days; and so, with many misgivings, he decided to try his hand at the law. Evening came on as he walked across the Massachusetts hills that December day, pursuing his solitary way, "lone wandering," "feeling forlorn and desolate" as he says in a published letter, and in the sky above him he beheld a wild duck that had become separated from the southward-winging flock and seemed to be wandering in its course. Doubtless the young poet said to himself, "I am like that wild duck; I, too, am wandering." That night he wrote *Lines to a Waterfowl*. The wild duck was an interpreter of the present meaning of life to him. From that day—when as a poor boy he was questioning what life had in store for him until he became recognized as the first citizen of New York, the founder of American poetry, and as Lincoln said, worth a trip across the continent to shake hands with—the lesson of trust expressed in the last stanza was his guiding motto. For sixty-three years—till his death in 1878—he held firmly to the faith of this poem of his youth.

TO A WATER-FOWL

1

Whither, midst falling dew,
While glow the heavens with the last steps of day,
Far, through their rosy depths, dost thou pursue
    Thy solitary way?

2

Vainly the fowler's eye
Might mark thy distant flight to do thee wrong,
As, darkly painted on the crimson sky,
　　Thy figure floats along.

3

Seek'st thou the plashy brink
Of weedy lake, or marge of river wide,
Or where the rocking billows rise and sink
　　On the chafed ocean side?

4

There is a Power whose care
Teaches thy way along that pathless coast,—
The desert and illimitable air,—
　　Lone wandering, but not lost.

5

All day thy wings have fanned,
At that far height, the cold, thin atmosphere,
Yet stoop not, weary, to the welcome land,
　　Though the dark night is near.

6

And soon that toil shall end.
Soon shalt thou find a summer home, and rest
And scream among thy fellows; reeds shall bend,
　　Soon. o'er thy sheltering nest.

FAMOUS POEMS EXPLAINED

7

Thou'rt gone, the abyss of heaven
Hath swallowed up thy form; yet, on my heart
Deeply hath sunk the lesson thou hast given,
    And shall not soon depart:

8

He who, from zone to zone,
Guides through the boundless sky thy certain flight,
In the long way that I must tread alone,
    Will lead my steps aright.
                —William Cullen Bryant.

Last steps of day—evening.

The second stanza simply means that the bird is too high for a hunter to shoot.

Plashy—watery; *marge*—margin.

Notice the striking contrast in the pictures presented in stanzas five and six. In the former the bird is wandering in a cold northern night; in the latter she is on her sheltered nest in the warm south.

Explain the migration of birds. Have you ever seen flocks of wild fowls?

The essence of the poem is found in the closing stanza. The emotion out of which the poem grew and which it in turn arouses is, of course, trust. "Poetry is the suggestion by the imagination of noble grounds for noble emotions." This poem illustrates the definition very well.

Read Whittier's *The Eternal Goodness*.

THE SANDPIPER

This beautiful little poem is not easily comprehended by one who has little or no knowledge of the seashore. The author of it lived nearly all of her life on one of the Isles of Shoals off the coast of New Hampshire. In reading it the inland student must use his imagination and picture clearly in his mind the scene described. He must create for himself, from pictures and descriptions, the scene which he has never beheld.

Imagine a little girl on the sandy ocean beach gathering the dry drift-wood for fuel, as a storm comes on. Running up and down the beach is a slender, long-legged bird similar to those that flit along some of our inland streams. The lighthouses are wrapt in the mists of the storm, and the ships have taken in their sails and are hurrying away to the harbor or to the deep open sea. It is a vivid picture, drawn with a few simple lines, of a rising storm on the seashore.

THE SANDPIPER

1

Across the narrow beach we flit,
  One little sandpiper and I;
And fast I gather, bit by bit,
  The scattered driftwood, bleached and dry.

The wild waves reach their hands for it,
  The wild wind raves, the tide runs high,
As up and down the beach we flit,
  One little sandpiper and I.

2

Above our heads the sullen clouds
  Scud black and swift across the sky;
Like silent ghosts in misty shrouds
  Stand out the white lighthouses high.
Almost as far as the eye can reach
  I see the close-reefed vessels fly,
As fast we flit along the beach,
  One little sandpiper and I.

3

I watch him as he skims along
  Uttering his sweet and mournful cry;
He starts not at my fitful song,
  Or flash of fluttering drapery.
He has no thought of any wrong;
  He scans me with a fearless eye.
Stanch friends are we, well-tried and strong,
  The little sandpiper and I.

4

Comrade, where wilt thou be to-night,
  When the loosed storm breaks furiously?
My driftwood fire will burn so bright!
  To what warm shelter canst thou fly?

I do not fear for thee, though wroth
   The tempest rushes through the sky;
For are we not God's children both,
   Thou, little sandpiper, and I?

                            —Celia Thaxter.

Those who have seen only coal or gas used as fuel will need to have the drift-wood, as fuel, explained to them.

The wild waves reach their hands for it. What does this sentence mean?

The tide runs high. Here is an opportunity to study, most effectively, the tides, and so combine reading and geography.

Just before a storm the sandpiper runs up and down the beach in the manner described in the poem. This is one of the signs of the coming storm.

Before the second stanza is read, be sure that you have a clear mental picture of the *sullen clouds* as they *scud black and swift across the sky.* Have you ever watched a storm come up? Describe it. Explain *sullen* as used here, and *scud.*

The third and fourth lines in stanza two make a striking picture. Miss Thaxter's father was for many years a lighthouse keeper on the Isles of Shoals. Show or draw a picture of a lighthouse and explain what lighthouses are for.

The third stanza indicates that the girl and the bird have been together so often and so much on the beach that they have come to know each other and to be friends.

Comrade. Why does she call the bird comrade? Are not the birds our little brothers of the field and the air? One who has ever loved a bird will give the word *comrade* a new meaning when he reads it here if it is explained to him.

The closing stanza is beautiful, both in the picture it presents and in the moral it teaches—the same moral that Bryant teaches in *Lines to a Water-fowl.*

THE REAPER AND THE FLOWERS

This poem, like most of Longfellow's, is easy to understand. *Bearded grain* refers to old people—shocks of corn fully ripe; and *the flowers that grow between* are the children. "They shall bloom in the fields of light," for "of such is the kingdom of heaven."

THE REAPER AND THE FLOWERS

1

There is a Reaper whose name is Death,
   And, with his sickle keen,
He reaps the bearded grain at a breath,
   And the flowers that grow between.

2

"Shall I have naught that is fair?" saith he;
   "Have naught but the bearded grain?
Though the breath of those flowers is sweet to me,
   I will give them all back again."

3

He gazed at the flowers with tearful eyes,
   He kissed their drooping leaves;
It was for the Lord of Paradise
   He bound them in his sheaves.

4

"My Lord has need of these flowerlets gay,"
  The Reaper said, and smiled;
"Dear tokens of the earth are they
  Where once he was a child.

5

"They shall all bloom in the fields of light,
  Transplanted by my care,
And saints, upon their garments white,
  These sacred blossoms wear."

6

And the mother gave in tears and pain
  The flowers she most did love;
She knew she should find them all again
  In the fields of light above.

7

O, not in cruelty, not in wrath,
  The Reaper came that day,
'T was an angel visited the green earth,
  And took the flowers away.

—Henry Wadsworth Longfellow.

DOWN TO SLEEP

This delightful little poem, read to a company of boys and girls roaming in the November woods, some clear, bright afternoon, will give a new meaning to the autumn-time, and a happy appreciation of the woods by the children. Select some pretty spot, have the children all sit down and try to be as still as the woods—then read to them in your most appreciative manner the first stanza of this poem. They will see that the woods are bare, they will feel the hushed silence of the forest, they will appreciate the warmth of the afternoon sun, and they will understand that all things are lying down to sleep for the winter. Before reading the second stanza, call their attention to the fresh, fragrant air of the woods. It is always the purest air in the world. Have the children feel with their hands the soft rich soil, into which the leaves are falling. Have them listen to the winds, the falling leaves, the cawing crows, or other forest sounds that are sure to break upon the November stillness of the woods. Then read, as before, the second stanza. Before reading the third stanza, have the children move about in the leafiest places, and scratch down among the leaves to the soil, to find the covered ferns, the acorns, the nuts and the seeds of maple, ash or elm. Let them dig in the loose, loamy soil, where the bulbs and tubers of violets, bloodroot, and hepaticas lie hidden under the "coverlids."

Seat the children again and read stanza three. Ask the children how they feel when they lie down to sleep. Are they glad or sad? Ask them how it makes them feel to think of all the plants lying down to sleep for the winter. The children might then be told that when we have lived our lives, we too, like the plants, must "lie down to sleep." Then read the fourth stanza, and finally read the entire poem through, so that its impression as a whole may rest upon and abide with you and the children like a benediction from the woods.

DOWN TO SLEEP

1

November woods are bare and still,
November days are clear and bright;
Each noon burns up the morning's chill,
The morning's snow is gone by night;
Each day my steps grow slow, grow light,
As through the woods I reverent creep,
Watching all things lie "down to sleep."

2

I never knew before what beds,
Fragrant to smell and soft to touch,
The forest sifts and shapes and spreads;
I never knew before how much
Of human sound there is in such
Low tones as through the forest sweep
When all wild things lie "down to sleep."

By permission of Little, Brown & Co.

3

Each day I find new coverlids
Tucked in, and more sweet eyes shut tight;
Sometimes the viewless mother bids
Her ferns kneel down full in my sight;
I hear their chorus of "Good-night!"
And half I smile and half I weep,
Listening while they lie "down to sleep."

4

November woods are bare and still,
November days are bright and good;
Life's noon burns up life's morning chill,
Life's night rests feet which long have stood;
Some warm, soft bed in field or wood
The mother will not fail to keep,
Where we can "lay us down to sleep."

—Helen Hunt Jackson.

THE BLUEBELL

The Bluebell tells a truth but not a fact; for there are many great truths which are not facts. Even some fairy stories contain great truths.

The little white flower, from constantly watching the sky and the star and longing for them, by and by became the color of the sky, with a tiny spot of gold in its

heart like the star. This was the origin of the color
of the Bluebell.

There is no better established fact in nature and in
life than this, that what one admires, longs for, strives
for, aspires to, he comes to resemble more and more;
he "takes their image by and by."

THE BLUEBELL

1

There is a story I have heard—
A poet learned it of a bird,
And kept its music every word—

2

A story of a dim ravine,
O'er which the towering treetops lean,
With one blue rift of sky between;

3

And there, two thousand years ago,
A little flower as white as snow
Swayed in the silence to and fro.

4

Day after day with longing eye,
The floweret watched the narrow sky,
And fleecy clouds that floated by.

5

And through the darkness, night by night,
One gleaming star would climb the height,
And cheer the lonely floweret's sight.

6

Thus, watching the blue heavens afar,
And the rising of its favorite star,
A slow change came—but not to mar;

7

For softly o'er its petals white
There crept a blueness, like the light
Of skies upon a summer night;

8

And in its chalice, I am told,
The bonny bell was formed to hold
A tiny star that gleamed like gold.

9

Now, little people sweet and true,
I find a lesson here for you
Writ in the floweret's bell of blue:

10

The patient child whose watchful eye
Strives after all things pure and high
Shall take their image by and by.

—Julia A. Eastman.

[*Note for the teacher:* Get the pupils to draw a picture of the scene described, no matter how crude their drawing may be. By attempting in this way to express their impressions of the scene they will get a better understanding of it. The dim ravine with towering treetops leaning over it, the streak of blue sky above with its one gleaming star of gold, and the little white flower at the bottom of the ravine constantly looking up to the sky and the star should be definitely imaged in their minds, otherwise they cannot really read the poem, no matter how glibly they may say the words.]

Hawthorne's story of *The Great Stone Face* should be read in connection with *The Bluebell*.

MAKE WAY FOR LIBERTY

The legend upon which this poem is founded is as follows, according to the *Encyclopedia Britannica:*

"The incident with which Arnold von Winkelried's name is connected is, after the feat of Tell, the best known and most popular in the early history of the Swiss Federation. We are told how, at a certain moment in the great battle of Sempach (July 9, 1386) when the Swiss had failed to break the serried ranks of the Austrian knights, a man of Unterwalden, Arnold von Winkelried by name, came to the rescue. Commending his wife and children to the care of his comrades, he rushed towards the Austrians, gathered a number of their spears together against his breast, and fell pierced through and through, having opened a way into the hostile ranks for his fellow countrymen, though at the price of his own life.

"The story has some solid ground to rest upon, and Winkelried's act might well have been performed, though as yet the amount of genuine and early evidence in support of it is very far from being sufficient."

The *American Cyclopedia* gives it as a historical fact.

The Austrians were very heavily armored in this battle, so that they resembled a "human wood," or a stone wall, each soldier being a "conscious stone," and they stood so close together that each seemed grown fast to "kindred thousands" of other armored knights (stanza two).

The Swiss were fighting to free their country from the oppression of the Austrians, and the incident retold in the poem is one of the most splendid and heroic in all the annals of patriotism.

MAKE WAY FOR LIBERTY

1

"Make way for Liberty!" he cried;
Made way for Liberty, and died!

2

In arms the Austrian phalanx stood,
A living wall, a human wood!
A wall, where every conscious stone
Seemed to its kindred thousands grown;

A rampart all assaults to bear,
Till time to dust their frames should wear;
A wood like that enchanted grove,
In which, with fiends, Rinaldo strove,
Where every silent tree possessed
A spirit prisoned in its breast,
Which the first stroke of coming strife
Would startle into hideous life:
So dense, so still, the Austrians stood,
A living wall, a human wood!

3

Impregnable their front appears,
All horrent with projected spears,
Whose polished points before them shine,
From flank to flank, one brilliant line,
Bright as the breakers' splendors run
Along the billows to the sun.

4

Opposed to these, a hovering band,
Contended for their native land;
Peasants, whose new-found strength had broke
From manly necks the ignoble yoke,
And forged their fetters into swords,
On equal terms to fight their lords;
And what insurgent rage had gained,
In many a mortal fray maintained:
Marshaled once more at Freedom's call,

They came to conquer or to fall,
Where he who conquered, he who fell,
Was deemed a dead, or living, Tell!

5

And now the work of life and death
Hung on the passing of a breath;
The fire of conflict burned within;
The battle trembled to begin;
Yet, while the Austrians held their ground,
Point for attack was nowhere found;
Where'er the impatient Switzers gazed,
The unbroken line of lances blazed;
That line 't were suicide to meet,
And perish at their tyrants' feet;
How could they rest within their graves,
And leave their homes the homes of slaves?
Would they not feel their children tread
With clanking chains above their head?

6

It must not be: this day, this hour,
Annihilates the oppressor's power;
All Switzerland is in the field,
She will not fly, she can not yield;
She must not fall; her better fate
Here gives her an immortal date.
Few were the numbers she could boast,

But every freeman was a host,
And felt as though himself were he
On whose sole arm hung victory.

7

It did depend on *one,* indeed:
Behold him! Arnold Winkelried!
There sounds not to the trump of fame
The echo of a nobler name.
Unmarked he stood amid the throng,
In rumination deep and long,
Till you might see, with sudden grace,
The very thought come o'er his face;
And by the motion of his form,
Anticipate the bursting storm;
And by the uplifting of his brow,
Tell where the bolt would strike, and how.
But 't was no sooner thought than done;
The field was in a moment won.

8

"Make way for Liberty!" he cried:
Then ran, with arms extended wide,
As if his dearest friend to clasp;
Ten spears he swept within his grasp:
"Make way for Liberty!" he cried,
Their keen points met from side to side;
He bowed amongst them like a tree,
And thus made way for Liberty.

9

Swift to the breach his comrades fly;
"Make way for Liberty!" they cry,
And through the Austrian phalanx dart,
As rushed the spears through Arnold's heart;
While instantaneous as his fall,
Rout, ruin, panic, scattered all.
An earthquake could not overthrow
A city with a surer blow.

10

Thus Switzerland again was free,
Thus Death made way for Liberty!

—James Montgomery.

Compare Tennyson's *Charge of the Light Brigade* (page 11), and the story of Thermopylæ.

THE RISING IN 1776

The Rising is based upon the following incident:

The pastor of the Lutheran church at Woodstock, in the Valley of Virginia, at the beginning of the American Revolution was John Peter Gabriel Muhlenberg, who had settled there in 1772. On the Sunday following the receipt of the news of the battle of Lexington and

THE RISING IN 1776

Concord he went into his pulpit wearing the full uniform of a colonel, but completely covered by his clerical gown. The sermon was a stirring one, in which he said there was a time to preach and a time to fight, and that the time to fight had come. Then he threw off his gown, read his commission as colonel, ordered the buglers and the drummers, whom he had stationed outside of the church, to sound the call to arms, and asked his congregation how many of them would volunteer. Many of them did so, and joined his regiment, the Eighth Virginia, afterward noted for its courage and good discipline. This regiment, led by the fighting preacher, participated in many important battles. Muhlenberg was made brigadier general, and major general at the close of the war. After the war he returned to his native state of Pennsylvania, served three terms in Congress, was elected to the United States Senate, was supervisor of revenues for the state, and held other offices.

The first four stanzas of the poem tell of the effect of the news from Lexington and Concord upon the people in the Valley of Virginia, and the rest of the poem is a free account of the occurrence mentioned above. Which Berkeley is referred to in verse nine is not clear, for Governor Berkeley, who might have uttered just such a sentiment, had been dead for a long time. Doubtless that incident is an embellishment introduced by the poet.

THE RISING IN 1776

1

Out of the North the wild news came,
Far flashing on its wings of flame,
Swift as the boreal light which flies
At midnight through the startled skies.

2

And there was tumult in the air,
  The fife's shrill note, the drum's loud beat,
And through the wide land everywhere
  The answering tread of hurrying feet;
While the first oath of Freedom's gun
Came on the blast from Lexington;
And Concord roused, no longer tame,
Forgot her old baptismal name,
Made bare her patriot arm of power,
And swelled the discord of the hour.

3

Within its shade of elm and oak
  The church of Berkeley Manor stood;
There Sunday found the rural folk,
  And some esteemed of gentle blood.
  In vain their feet with loitering tread
Passed 'mid the graves where rank is naught;
All could not read the lesson taught
  In that republic of the dead.

4

How sweet the hour of Sabbath talk,
  The vale with peace and sunshine full
Where all the happy people walk,
  Decked in their homespun flax and wool!

*   *   *   *   *

5

The pastor rose: the prayer was strong;
The psalm was warrior David's song;
The text, a few short words of might,—
"The Lord of hosts shall arm the right!"

6

He spoke of wrongs too long endured,
Of sacred rights to be secured;
Then from his patriot tongue of flame
The startling words for Freedom came.
The stirring sentences he spake
Compelled the heart to glow or quake,
And, rising on his theme's broad wing,
  And grasping in his nervous hand
  The imaginary battle-brand,
In face of death he dared to fling
Defiance to a tyrant king.

7

Even as he spoke, his frame, renewed
In eloquence of attitude,

Rose, as it seemed, a shoulder higher;
Then swept his kindling glance of fire
From startled pew to breathless choir;
When suddenly his mantle wide
His hands impatient flung aside,
And, lo! he met their wondering eyes
Complete in all a warrior's guise.

8

A moment there was awful pause,—
When Berkeley cried, "Cease, traitor, cease!
God's temple is the house of peace!"

The other shouted, "Nay, not so,
When God is with our righteous cause;
His holiest places then are ours,
His temples are our forts and towers

That frown upon the tyrant foe;
In this, the dawn of Freedom's day,
There is a time to fight and pray!"

9

And now before the open door—
  The warrior priest had ordered so—
The enlisting trumpet's sudden roar
Rang through the chapel, o'er and o'er
  Its long reverberating blow
So loud and clear, it seemed the ear
Of dusty death must wake and hear.
And there the startling drum and fife

Fired the living with fiercer life;
While overhead, with wild increase,
Forgetting its ancient toll of peace,
  The great bell swung as ne'er before:
It seemed as it would never cease;
And every word its ardor flung
From off its jubilant iron tongue
  Was "War! WAR! WAR!"

10

"Who dares"—this was the patriot's cry,
  As striding from the desk he came—
  "Come out with me, in Freedom's name,
For her to live, for her to die?"
A hundred hands flung up reply,
A hundred voices answered *"I!"*

—Thomas Buchanan Read.

Poured . . . the lead into the molds of death—molded bullets.

Republic of the dead—the cemetery, where high and low at last are equal.

Concord means harmony, peace (stanza two).

Warrior David's song may possibly refer to *Psalm 20.*

THE SINGING LESSON

So perfect a songster as the nightingale once made a mistake and sang a false note. Sensitive soul that she was, she grieved over the mistake and thought she would never sing any more. She knew that the other birds were criticizing her and sneering at her. A kind-hearted dove told her that she was foolish to take the matter so seriously: "Only think of all you have done, only think of all you can do." Encouraged by these kind words the nightingale forgot her critics, fixed her eyes on the skies, and sang such a song that the birds stopped in their passage to listen and the people stood still below to hear the wonderful psalm.

Transfer this fable from the bird kingdom to the human kingdom and the significance is clear. Even the best is likely to make a mistake. It may be a small thing compared with all the rest that that life stands for. But there will be plenty of sneers and criticisms—often from jealous persons, as the lark and the thrush were jealous of the nightingale.

The kind words of a friend may make one take courage once more. And if he fixes his aim on the higher things and pays no attention to his critics, jealous or otherwise, his later work will be even better than his former.

THE SINGING LESSON

1

A nightingale made a mistake;
    She sang a few notes out of tune:
Her heart was ready to break,
    And she hid away from the moon.

She wrung her claws, poor thing,
　But was far too proud to weep;
She tucked her head under her wing,
　And pretended to be asleep.

2

A lark, arm in arm with a thrush,
　Came sauntering up to the place;
The nightingale felt herself blush,
　Though feathers hid her face;
She knew they had heard her song,
　She felt them snicker and sneer;
She thought that life was too long,
　And wished she could skip a year.

3

"O nightingale!" cooed a dove;
　"O nightingale! what's the use?
You bird of beauty and love,
　Why behave like a goose?
Don't sulk away from our sight,
　Like a common, contemptible fowl;
You bird of joy and delight,
　Why behave like an owl?

4

"Only think of all you have done;
　Only think of all you can do;

A false note is really fun
  From such a bird as you!
Lift up your proud little crest,
  Open your musical beak;
Other birds have to do their best,
  You need only to speak!"

5

The nightingale shyly took
  Her head from under her wing,
And, giving the dove a look,
  Straightway began to sing.
There was never a bird could pass;
  The night was divinely calm;
And the people stood on the grass
  To hear that wonderful psalm.

6

The nightingale did not care,
  She sang only to the skies;
Her song ascended there,
  And there she fixed her eyes.
The people that stood below
  She knew but little about;
And this tale has a moral, I know,
  If you'll try and find it out.

—Jean Ingelow.

FAITHLESS NELLY GRAY

This is a poem of puns. A pun is the lowest order of wit, but some of these are exceedingly clever. Every stanza has a play on the double meaning of words or phrases, and these double meanings should be sought out. For example, the last word in the tenth stanza might be spelled either "Nell" or "Knell," for the author intends it to have both of these meanings. In the twelfth stanza, the last word means both the infantry and the rope with which the soldier is about to hang himself. The reader should study out all of these double meanings or puns—there are more than a dozen of them—for the poem is simply an exercise in turning words to eccentric uses. A list of these verbal twists might be made. There is nothing else of value in the piece. "Forty-second Foot," in stanza two, means the Forty-second Company of Infantry.

FAITHLESS NELLY GRAY

1

Ben Battle was a soldier bold,
  And used to war's alarms;
But a cannon ball took off his legs,
  So he laid down his arms!

2

Now, as they bore him off the field,
  Said he, "Let others shoot,
For here I leave my second leg,
  And the Forty-second Foot!"

3

The army surgeons made him limbs;
  Said he, "They're only pegs;
But there's as wooden members quite,
  As represent my legs!"

4

Now Ben, he loved a pretty maid,
  Her name was Nelly Gray;
So he went to pay her his *devours,*
  When he'd devoured his pay.

5

But when he called on Nelly Gray,
  She made him quite a scoff;
And when she saw his wooden legs,
  Began to take them off!

6

"O Nelly Gray! O Nelly Gray!
  Is this your love so warm?
The love that loves a scarlet coat
  Should be more uniform!"

FAITHLESS NELLY GRAY

7

Said she, "I loved a soldier once,
  For he was blithe and brave;
But I will never have a man
  With both legs in the grave!

8

"Before you had these timber toes,
  Your love I did allow,
But then, you know, you stand upon
  Another footing now!"

*   *   *   *   *   *

9

"O false and fickle Nelly Gray!
  I know why you refuse:
Though I've no feet—some other man
  Is standing in my shoes!

10

"I wish I ne'er had seen your face;
  But, now, a long farewell!
For you will be my death;—alas!
  You will not be my Nell!"

11

Now when he went from Nelly Gray,
  His heart so heavy got,
And life was such a burden grown,
  It made him take a knot!

12

So round his melancholy neck
　A rope he did entwine,
And for the second time in life
　Enlisted in the Line!

13

One end he tied around a beam,
　And then removed his pegs,
And, as his legs were off, of course
　He soon was off his legs.

14

And there he hung till he was dead
　As any nail in town;
For, though distress had cut him up,
　It could not cut him down!

　　　　　　　　　—Thomas Hood.

BURIAL OF SIR JOHN MOORE

Sir John Moore, commanding the British forces in Spain in the war with Napoleon, was killed at the battle of Corunna, Spain, January 16, 1809. The battle occurred at the end of a long and hard retreat, and although the English had the advantage, they embarked at Corunna after the battle and returned to England.

The French forces were under Marshal Soult. Alison's *History of Europe* says that Moore "was wrapped by his attendants in his military cloak and laid in a grave hastily formed on the ramparts of Corunna, where a monument was soon after erected over his uncoffined remains by the generosity of the French Marshal Ney. Not a word was spoken as the melancholy interment by torchlight took place; silently they laid him in his grave, while the distant cannon of the battlefield fired the funeral honors to his memory.

"This tomb, originally erected by the French, since enlarged by the British, bears a simple but touching inscription, written of the hero over whose remains it is placed. Few spots in Europe will ever be more the object of general interest. His very misfortunes were the means which procured him immortal fame—his disastrous retreat, bloody death, and finally his tomb on a foreign strand, far from home and friends. There is scarcely a Spaniard but has heard of his tomb and speaks of it with a strange kind of awe."

Many fantastic legends have grown up among the Spanish people about the tomb and about the manner of the death of the great soldier.

The inscription on the tomb is as follows:

JOHN MOORE
LEADER OF THE ENGLISH ARMIES
SLAIN IN BATTLE, 1809.

But it is safe to say that the exquisite little poem, *The Burial of Sir John Moore,* by Rev. Charles Wolfe, has done more to perpetuate the name and fame of Moore than all other things combined.

BURIAL OF SIR JOHN MOORE

1

Not a drum was heard, nor a funeral note,
  As his corse to the rampart we hurried;
Not a soldier discharged his farewell shot
  O'er the grave where our hero we buried.

2

We buried him darkly, at dead of night,
  The sods with our bayonets turning;
By the struggling moonbeams' misty light,
  And the lantern dimly burning.

3

No useless coffin enclosed his breast,
  Nor in sheet nor in shroud we wound him;
But he lay, like a warrior taking his rest,
  With his martial cloak around him.

4

Few and short were the prayers we said,
  And we spoke not a word of sorrow;
But we steadfastly gazed on the face of the dead,
  And we bitterly thought of the morrow.

5

We thought, as we hollowed his narrow bed,
  And smoothed down his lonely pillow,
That the foe and the stranger would tread o'er his head,
  And we far away on the billow!

6

Lightly they'll talk of the spirit that's gone,
  And o'er his cold ashes upbraid him;
But little he'll reck, if they let him sleep on,
  In the grave where a Briton has laid him!

7

But half of our heavy task was done,
  When the clock tolled the hour for retiring;
And we heard the distant and random gun
  That the foe was sullenly firing.

8

Slowly and sadly we laid him down,
  From the field of his fame fresh and gory!
We carved not a line, we raised not a stone,
  But we left him alone in his glory.

—Charles Wolfe.

THE BURIAL OF MOSES

The Burial of Moses is based upon the following beautiful verses from the thirty-fourth chapter of *Deuteronomy:*

1. And Moses went up from the plains of Moab unto the mountain of Nebo, to the top of Pisgah, that is over against Jericho. And the Lord shewed him all the land of Gilead, unto Dan,

2. And all Naphtali, and the land of Ephraim, and Manasseh, and all the land of Judah, unto the utmost sea,

3. And the south, and the plain of the valley of Jericho, the city of palm trees, unto Zoar.

4. And the Lord said unto him, This *is* the land which I sware unto Abraham, unto Isaac, and unto Jacob, saying, I will give it unto thy seed: I have caused thee to see *it* with thine eyes, but thou shalt not go over thither.

5. So Moses the servant of the Lord died there in the land of Moab, according to the word of the Lord.

6. And he buried him in a valley in the land of Moab, over against Beth-peor: but no man knoweth of his sepulchre unto this day.

7. And Moses was a hundred and twenty years old when he died: his eye was not dim, nor his natural force abated.

8. And the children of Israel wept for Moses in the plains of Moab thirty days: so the days of weeping *and* mourning for Moses were ended.

THE BURIAL OF MOSES

1

By Nebo's lonely mountain,
  There lies a lonely grave;
In a vale in the land of Moab,
  On this side Jordan's wave,

THE BURIAL OF MOSES

And no man knows that sepulchre,
  And no man saw it e'er,
For the angels of God upturned the sod,
  And laid the dead man there.

2

That was the grandest funeral
  That ever passed on earth;
But no man heard the trampling,
  Or saw the train go forth,—
Noiselessly as the daylight
  Comes back when night is done,
And the crimson streaks on ocean's cheek
  Grow into the great sun,—

3

Noiselessly as the springtime
  Her crown of verdure weaves,
And all the trees on all the hills
  Open their thousand leaves;
So without sound of music,
  Or voice of them that wept,
Silently down from the mountain's crown
  The great procession swept.

4

Perchance the bald old eagle,
  On gray Beth-peor's height,
Out of his lonely eyrie,
  Looked on the wondrous sight;

Perchance the lion stalking
  Still shuns that hallowed spot,
For beast and bird have seen and heard
  That which man knoweth not.

5

But when the warrior dieth,
  His comrades in the war,
With arms reversed and muffled drum,
  Follow his funeral car;
They show the banners taken,
  They tell his battles won,
And after him lead his masterless steed,
  While peals the minute gun.

6

Amid the noblest of the land
  We lay the sage to rest,
And give the bard an honored place
  With costly marble drest,
In the great minster transept
  Where lights like glories fall,
And the organ rings, and the sweet choir sings,
  Along the emblazoned wall.

*   *   *   *   *   *   *

7

In that strange grave without a name,
  Whence his uncoffined clay

Shall break again, O wondrous thought!
  Before the Judgment Day,
And stand, with glory wrapt around,
  On the hills he never trod,
And speak of the strife that won our life,
  With the Incarnate Son of God.

8

O lonely grave in Moab's land!
  O dark Beth-peor's hill!
Speak to these curious hearts of ours,
  And teach them to be still.
God hath his mysteries of grace,
  Ways that we cannot tell;
He hides them deep, like the hidden sleep
  Of Him He loved so well.

—Cecil Frances Alexander.

THE AMERICAN FLAG

Drake's familiar poem is a little sophomorical, but it is worthy of the place it holds in the school Readers.

The people of mountainous countries have always been supposed to be more zealous for their freedom than dwellers in the low countries, and this is why the author puts Freedom on the mountain top (first line). He fancies that the colors in the flag all came from the sky—the blue from the azure robe (the sky), the white

from the Milky Way, the red from the streakings of
the sunrise, and the stars from the stars of the heavens.

THE AMERICAN FLAG

When Freedom, from her mountain height
   Unfurled her standard to the air,
She tore the azure robe of night,
   And set the stars of glory there!
She mingled with its gorgeous dyes
The milky baldric of the skies,
And striped its pure celestial white
With streakings of the morning light;
Then, from his mansion in the sun,
She called her eagle-bearer down,
And gave into his mighty hand
The symbol of her chosen land.

    *   *   *   *   *

Flag of the brave! thy folds shall fly,
The sign of hope and triumph, high,
When speaks the signal trumpet tone,
And the long line comes gleaming on;
Ere yet the lifeblood, warm and wet,
Has dimmed the glistening bayonet,
Each soldier's eye shall brightly turn
To where thy sky-born glories burn.
And, as his springing steps advance,
Catch war and vengeance from the glance.
And when the cannon-mouthings loud

Heave in wild wreaths the battle shroud,
And gory sabres rise and fall
Like shoots of flame on midnight's pall,
Then shall thy meteor glances glow,
   And cowering foes shall shrink beneath
Each gallant arm that strikes below
   That lovely messenger of death.

   *   *   *   *   *   *

Flag of the free heart's hope and home,
   By angel hands to valor given,
Thy stars have lit the welkin dome,
   And all thy hues were born in heaven.
Forever float that standard sheet!
   Where breathes the foe but falls before us,
With Freedom's soil beneath our feet,
   And Freedom's banner streaming o'er us?

—Joseph Rodman Drake.

Milky baldric refers to the Milky Way in the sky, *baldric* meaning a band or sash.

In the tenth line, *eagle* is represented as the flag bearer. The flag is frequently represented as being clutched in the talons of the American eagle—*his mighty hand* here meaning the eagle's claws.

From his mansion in the sun has reference to the fact that the eagle builds his nest at the highest points.

Battle shroud—the smoke of battle.

Meteor glances—flashings from the flag (not a very good figure, by the way).

By angel hands to valor given refers to the poetic origin of the colors of the flag in heaven as stated in the first eight lines, and as repeated in the following two lines. The poem closes with a declaration, in question form, that there is no foe anywhere who must not fall before us as we stand with Freedom's soil beneath our feet and the stars and stripes floating over us.

OLD IRONSIDES

Old Ironsides was the frigate *Constitution*. She was launched at Boston in 1797, took part in the bombardment of Tripoli in 1804, and made a great record in the War of 1812, capturing many vessels. One of her most notable engagements was with the British *Guerriere* off the Gulf of St. Lawrence. Her good fortune was remarkable throughout her service. "She never was dismasted, never got ashore, and scarcely ever suffered any of the usual accidents of the sea." Consequently she became a great favorite in the popular mind.

One day, not long after Holmes's graduation from Harvard, he read in a newspaper that the Secretary of the Navy had issued orders for the breaking up of the *Constitution,* then lying at Charlestown harbor, near Boston. Immediately he wrote his stirring protest in the lines of *Old Ironsides*. Throughout the country the press copied the poem, it met a quick response in the hearts of the people, the Secretary of the Navy revoked his order, and the gallant ship was saved.

In 1906 the Secretary of the Navy suggested that *Old Ironsides* be used as a practice target for the guns of the navy, but the newspapers in all parts of the country raised such a loud and such a general protest that the suggestion was never carried into effect and the proud old ship today lies in the Boston navy-yard "housed over."

OLD IRONSIDES

1

Ay, tear her tattered ensign down!
  Long has it waved on high,
And many an eye has danced to see
  That banner in the sky;
Beneath it rung the battle shout,
  And burst the cannon's roar;—
The meteor of the ocean air
  Shall sweep the clouds no more!

2

Her deck, once red with heroes' blood,
  Where knelt the vanquished foe,
When winds were hurrying o'er the flood,
  And waves were white below,
No more shall feel the victor's tread,
  Or know the conquered knee;—
The harpies of the shore shall pluck
  The eagle of the sea!

3

O better that her shattered hulk
  Should sink beneath the wave;
Her thunders shook the mighty deep
  And there should be her grave;
Nail to the mast her holy flag,
  Set every threadbare sail,
And give her to the god of storms,
  The lightning and the gale!

—Oliver Wendell Holmes.

Notice the striking figures of speech in *The meteor of the ocean air, The harpies of the shore,* and *The eagle of the sea. Harpies* here means plunderers.

The last four lines present a particularly fine picture, which the reader should re-create in his imagination.

THE BATTLE OF BLENHEIM

Southey here gives us a fine piece of sarcasm. It is in fact a most severe criticism of war, although pretending to praise its glories. Many thousand men fell at the battle of Blenheim—but it was a "great victory!" Nobody knows just why they killed each other—but it was a "famous victory!" Women and children were slain—but it was a "famous victory!" Many thousand bodies lay rotting in the sun—but it was a "famous victory!" Nobody knows what good came of it—but it was a "famous victory!" The battle of Blenheim

THE BATTLE OF BLENHEIM

was a "very wicked thing," as most battles have been, but it was a "famous victory!" The sarcasm throughout the poem is cutting and terrible.

The speakers in the poem are an old farmer named Kaspar, whose home is near Blenheim in Bavaria, and his two little grandchildren, one of whom brings in a human skull which he has found on the battlefield, and wants to know what it is. This skull serves as the text for the dialogue that follows—a dialogue on the horrors and wickedness of war as represented in the "famous victory" of Blenheim.

The battle of Blenheim was indeed the most famous victory of England's most famous general, the Duke of Marlborough, "who never fought a battle that he did not win, and never besieged a place that he did not take." The battle was fought August 13, 1704, during the "War of the Spanish Succession," which lasted ten years and was caused by the jealousy of European monarchs. The common people knew little or nothing about the cause of it, and doubtless cared little or nothing. England, Germany, Holland, Prussia and other powers formed the "Grand Alliance" to keep France and Spain from being united under one monarch. The war that followed was "literally universal," as Schwill says, "and raged at one and the same time at all the exposed points of the French-Spanish possessions, that is, in the Spanish Netherlands, along the upper Rhine, in Italy, in Spain itself, on the sea, and in the colonies of North America." During the progress of the war the emperor of Germany died and was succeeded by his brother, Charles VI. Now this same Charles was the prince whom the Grand Alliance was trying to put on the throne of Spain. To have Germany and Spain under one monarch would be as bad as to have France and Spain under one monarch—so England and Holland thought, and this new jealousy made the Grand Alliance go to pieces. The peace of Utrecht, 1713, followed, by which the Spanish dominions were divided. Everybody managed to get a share of the booty, England's share being the French possessions in North America, namely, Newfoundland, Nova Scotia, the Hudson Bay territory; together with the Spanish rock of Gibraltar, which gave her the command of the Mediterranean sea.

To this day it has not been settled who was really entitled to the crown of Spain—but the battle of Blenheim was a "famous victory!"

THE BATTLE OF BLENHEIM

1

It was a summer evening,
  Old Kaspar's work was done,
And he, before his cottage door,
  Was sitting in the sun;
And by him sported on the green
His little grandchild Wilhelmine.

2

She saw her brother Peterkin
  Roll something large and round,
Which he beside the rivulet,
  In playing there, had found;
He came to ask what he had found
That was so large, and smooth, and round.

3

Old Kaspar took it from the boy,
  Who stood expectant by;
And then the old man shook his head,
  And, with a natural sigh,
" 'T is some poor fellow's skull," said he,
"Who fell in the great victory.

4

"I find them in the garden,
  For there's many hereabout;
And often when I go to plow,
  The plowshare turns them out;
For many thousand men," said he,
"Were slain in that great victory."

5

"Now tell us what 't was all about,"
  Young Peterkin he cries;

While little Wilhelmine looks up
   With wonder-waiting eyes;
"Now tell us all about the war,
And what they killed each other for."

6

"It was the English," Kaspar cried,
   "Who put the French to rout,
But what they killed each other for,
   I could not well make out;
But everybody said," quoth he,
"That 't was a famous victory.

7

"My father lived at Blenheim then,
   Yon little stream, hard by;
They burnt his dwelling to the ground,
   And he was forced to fly;
So, with his wife and child he fled,
Nor had he where to rest his head.

8

"With fire and sword the country round
   Was wasted far and wide,
And many a childing mother there,
   And new-born baby died;

But things like that, you know, must be
At every famous victory.

9

"They say it was a shocking sight
  After the field was won;
For many thousand bodies here
  Lay rotting in the sun;
But things like that, you know, must be
After a famous victory.

10

"Great praise the Duke of Marlbro' won,
  And our good Prince Eugene;"
"Why 't was a very wicked thing!"
  Said little Wilhelmine.
"Nay, nay, my little girl," quoth he,
"It was a famous victory.

11

"And everybody praised the Duke
  Who this great fight did win."
"But what good came of it at last?"
  Quoth little Peterkin.
"Why, that I cannot tell," said he,
"But 't was a famous victory."

—Robert Southey.

COLUMBUS

To read this inspiring poem with the understanding one must think of the dangers of the voyage—of how the sailors thought the sea was filled with awful monsters, of how they threatened to throw Columbus overboard if he did not take them back home, and of the matchless courage of Columbus. These things are best revealed in the journal or diary kept by Columbus. In it he speaks of himself in the third person, as the Admiral, and he begins every day's journal with the simple statement that that day he sailed westward. Then follows an account of the terrors of the trip; but the next day's journal starts off calmly with the statement that that day he sailed westward. No mutiny of the sailors and no horror of the seas could keep him from sailing westward, for that was his course. Joaquin Miller has caught the spirit of the heroic event and put it into stirring rhyme. Here are four brief extracts from the Columbus journal:

THURSDAY, Sept. 13, 1492.

That day and night, steering their course, which was west, they made 33 leagues. . . . The currents were against them. On this day at the commencement of the night, the needles turned a half point to north-west, and in the morning they turned somewhat more north-west.

[Elsewhere he notes that this variation had never been observed by anyone up to that time, and that it caused much consternation among the sailors.]

SATURDAY, Sept. 15, 1492.

That day and night they made 27 leagues and rather more on their west course; and in the early part of the night there fell from heaven into the sea a marvelous flame of fire, at a distance of about 4 or 5 leagues from them.

WEDNESDAY, Oct. 10, 1492.

He sailed west-southwest. . . . Here the crew could stand it no longer. They complained of the long voyage, but the Admiral encouraged them as best he could, giving them hopes of the profits they might have. And he added that it was useless to murmur, because he had come in quest of the Indies, and was going to continue until he found them, with God's help.

THURSDAY, October 11, 1492.

He sailed to the west-southwest, but a high sea, higher than hitherto. . . . The Admiral at ten o'clock at night, standing on the castle of the poop, saw a light, but so indistinct that he did not dare to affirm that it was land; yet he called the attention of Pedro Gutierrez, a king's butler, to it and told him that it seemed to be a light, and told him to look; he did so and saw it. . . . After the Admiral said this it was seen once or twice, and it was like a small wax candle that was being hoisted and raised. . . . The Admiral, however, was quite convinced of the proximity of land. . . . Two hours after midnight the land appeared two leagues off.

COLUMBUS

1

Behind him lay the gray Azores,
 Behind the Gates of Hercules;
Before him not the ghost of shores,
 Before him only shoreless seas.

The good mate said: "Now must we pray,
   For lo! the very stars are gone.
Brave Adm'r'l, speak, what shall I say?"
   "Why, say: 'Sail on! sail on! and on!'"

2

"My men grow mutinous day by day;
   My men grow ghastly wan and weak."
The stout mate thought of home; a spray
   Of salt wave washed his swarthy cheek.
"What shall I say, brave Adm'r'l, say,
   If we sight naught but seas at dawn?"
"Why, you shall say at break of day:
   'Sail on! sail on! sail on! and on!'"

They sailed and sailed, as winds might blow,
   Until at last the blanched mate said:
"Why, now not even God would know
   Should I and all my men fall dead.
These very winds forget their way,
   For God from these dread seas is gone.
Now speak, brave Adm'r'l, speak and say."—
   He said: "Sail on! sail on! and on!"

4

They sailed. They sailed. Then spake the mate:
   "This mad sea shows his teeth to-night.
He curls his lip, he lies in wait,
   With lifted teeth, as if to bite!

Brave Adm'r'l, say but one good word:
  What shall we do when hope is gone?"
The words leapt like a leaping sword:
  "Sail on! sail on! sail on! and on!"

5

Then, pale and worn, he kept his deck,
  And peered through darkness. Ah, that night
Of all dark nights! And then a speck—
  A light! A light! A light! A light!
It grew, a starlit flag unfurled!
  It grew to be Time's burst of dawn.
He gained a world; he gave that world
  Its grandest lesson: "On! sail on!"

—Joaquin Miller.

In *stanza four*, notice the description of a fierce storm at sea. Columbus says in his journal for October 11 that they had a high sea that day, "higher than hitherto."

He kept his deck and peered through darkness—Columbus watched all night and was the first to see a light. If possible, his feelings should be imagined in reading of this momentous event in the world's history.

A starlit flag unfurled—A part of the land discovered by him became the United States with its stars and stripes.

Time's burst of dawn—a new era in the world's history.

The poem should be read by the members of the history classes in their study of the period of discovery. One who does not endeavor to bring into play a vivid imagination cannot read it with full understanding and pleasure.

CHICAGO: OCTOBER 10, 1871

The reference is, of course, to the Chicago fire, in which nearly one hundred thousand people were rendered homeless, more than three square miles were burned over, and property worth more than two hundred million dollars was destroyed. Chicago had grown up so rapidly that it is compared to Aladdin's palace, which was created in a night, as told in the *Arabian Nights*. The cry of Macedonia to Paul, in the Bible, was "come over and help us." All the civilized world responded generously to Chicago's cry for help. "The silver cup hid in the proffered meal" has reference to Joseph's putting his silver cup in his brother Benjamin's sack of corn. *Genesis 44;* 1-2, reads:

1. And he commanded the steward of his house, saying, Fill the men's sacks *with* food, as much as they can carry, and put every man's money in his sack's mouth:
2. And put my cup, the silver cup, in the sack's mouth of the youngest, and his corn money. And he did according to the word that Joseph had spoken.

CHICAGO: OCTOBER 10, 1871

1

Blackened and bleeding, helpless, panting prone,
On the charred fragments of her shattered throne
Lies she who stood but yesterday alone.

2

Queen of the West! by some enchanter taught
To lift the glory of Aladdin's court,
Then lose the spell that all that wonder wrought.

3

Like her own prairies by some chance seed sown,
Like her own prairies in one brief day grown,
Like her own prairies in one fierce night mown.

4

She lifts her voice, and in her pleading call
We hear her cry of Macedon to Paul,
The cry for help that makes her kin to all.

5

But haply with wan fingers may she feel
The silver cup hid in the proffered meal,
The gifts her kinship and our love reveal.

—Bret Harte.

In one fierce night mown—has reference to prairie fires.

THE WRECK OF THE HESPERUS

The Wreck of the Hesperus is an imitation of the old English ballads in both spirit and form. Following the custom of the old ballad writers, Longfellow, in order to make the meter right, makes the accent fall upon the last syllable of "daughter" in the first verse, "sailor" in the fourth verse, and "daughter" in the eighth.

Norman's Woe is the name of a dangerous reef off the coast of Gloucester, Mass. In December, 1839, an issue of the Boston *Advertiser* published an account of a vessel, *The Hesperus,* wrecked off this reef, with a woman's form lashed to the mast. About a fortnight later, after a violent storm, Longfellow rose in the middle of the night and wrote the poem in less than an hour. The detail of the ballad is, of course, his own invention.

THE WRECK OF THE HESPERUS

1

It was the schooner Hesperus,
  That sailed the wintry sea;
And the skipper had taken his little daughtér,
  To bear him company.

2

Blue were her eyes as the fairy-flax,
  Her cheeks like the dawn of day,
And her bosom white as the hawthorn buds,
  That ope in the month of May.

THE WRECK OF THE HESPERUS

3

The skipper he stood beside the helm,
  His pipe was in his mouth,
And he watched how the veering flaw did blow
  The smoke now West, now South.

4

Then up and spake an old sailór,
  Had sailed to the Spanish Main,
"I pray thee, put into yonder port,
  For I fear a hurricane.

5

"Last night, the moon had a golden ring,
  And to-night no moon we see!"
The skipper, he blew a whiff from his pipe,
  And a scornful laugh laughed he.

6

Colder and louder blew the wind,
  A gale from the Northeast,
The snow fell hissing in the brine,
  And the billows frothed like yeast.

7

Down came the storm, and smote amain
  The vessel in its strength;
She shuddered and paused, like a frighted steed,
  Then leaped her cable's length.

8

"Come hither! come hither! my little daughtér,
   And do not tremble so;
For I can weather the roughest gale
   That ever wind did blow."

9

He wrapped her warm in his seaman's coat
   Against the stinging blast;
He cut a rope from a broken spar,
   And bound her to the mast.

10

"O father! I hear the church bells ring,
   O say, what may it be?"
" 'T is a fog bell on a rock-bound coast!"—
   And he steered for the open sea.

11

"O father! I hear the sound of guns,
   O say, what may it be?"
"Some ship in distress, that cannot live
   In such an angry sea!"

12

"O father! I see the gleaming light,
   O say, what may it be?"
But the father answered never a word,
   A frozen corpse was he.

13

Lashed to the helm, all stiff and stark,
  With his face turned to the skies,
The lantern gleamed through the gleaming snow
  On his fixed and glassy eyes.

14

Then the maiden clasped her hands and prayed
  That savèd she might be;
And she thought of Christ, who stilled the wave,
  On the Lake of Galilee.

15

And fast through the midnight dark and drear,
  Through the whistling sleet and snow,
Like a sheeted ghost, the vessel swept
  Tow'rds the reef of Norman's Woe.

16

And ever the fitful gusts between
  A sound came from the land;
It was the sound of the trampling surf
  On the rocks and the hard sea-sand.

17

The breakers were right beneath her bows,
  She drifted a dreary wreck,
And a whooping billow swept the crew
  Like icicles from her deck.

18

She struck where the white and fleecy waves
    Looked soft as carded wool,
But the cruel rocks, they gored her side
    Like the horns of an angry bull.

19

Her rattling shrouds, all sheathed in ice,
    With the masts went by the board;
Like a vessel of glass, she strove and sank,
    Ho! ho! the breakers roared!

20

At daybreak, on the bleak sea-beach,
    A fisherman stood aghast,
To see the form of a maiden fair,
    Lashed close to a drifting mast.

21

The salt sea was frozen on her breast,
    The salt tears in her eyes;
And he saw her hair, like the brown seaweed,
    On the billows fall and rise.

22

Such was the wreck of the Hesperus,
    In the midnight and the snow!
Christ, save us all from a death like this,
    On the reef of Norman's Woe!

                —Henry Wadsworth Longfellow.

Spanish main—the name formerly given to the southern portion of the Caribbean sea.

Skipper—the master, or captain, of a vessel.

Flaw—a sudden gust of wind.

Bound her to the mast—to keep the storm from throwing her into the sea.

What she took to be the church bells, the sound of guns, and the gleaming light, were danger or distress signals.

With the captain frozen to death at his post of duty, where he had tied himself to keep from going overboard, there was nothing to keep the ship from being driven by the storm against the rocks.

Stanza seven is particularly fine:

> Down came the storm and smote amain
> The vessel in its strength;
> She shuddered and paused, like a frighted steed,
> Then leaped her cable's length.

So also is stanza eighteen:

> She struck where the white and fleecy waves
> Looked soft as carded wool,
> But the cruel rocks they gored her side
> Like the horns of an angry bull.

KING SOLOMON AND THE ANTS

This poem is an allegory founded upon a legend. Legends almost innumerable grew up about the great character of Solomon. These legends are preserved in the Koran, the Talmud, and other oriental books. Many of the most interesting of them are about his conversations with birds, insects, and animals. Solomon was supposed to know their languages. The legend upon which Whittier based his poem of *Solomon and the Ants* is doubtless the following, which is found in the Koran:

> And Solomon inherited from David the gift of prophecy and knowledge; and he said, "O men, I have been taught the language of birds, and have had bestowed on me of everything wherewith prophets and kings are gifted." And his armies of jinn (demons) and men and birds were gathered together unto Solomon, and they were led on in order, until, when they came unto the valley of ants, which was at Et-Taif in Syria, the queen of the ants, having seen the troops of Solomon, said, "O ants, enter your habitations, lest Solomon and his troops crush you violently, while they perceive not." And Solomon smiled, afterwards laughing at her saying, which he heard from the distance of three miles, the wind conveying it to him; so he withheld his forces when he came in sight of their valley, until the ants had entered their dwellings. And his troops were on horses and on foot in this expedition.

So much for the legend. The meaning of the allegory is this: The ants represent the multitudes of common people—the masses; the king and queen represent the rich and powerful. The ants (the common people) think that the rich and powerful crush them to death without even paying any attention. The queen, representing a certain type of rich and powerful people still to be found in every country, says that these ants (common people) ought to be thankful to be trampled upon by so great a king—it is a great honor to them if they only knew it! But Solomon, representing true greatness, tells her that the wise and strong should seek the welfare of the weak. And his train followed his example (such a leader is always followed) and spared the life, liberty, and homes of the poor folk. It is a beautiful legend and a profitable allegory.

KING SOLOMON AND THE ANTS

1

Out from Jerusalem
  The king rode with his great
  War chiefs and lords of state,
And Sheba's queen with them.

2

Proud in the Syrian sun,
  In gold and purple sheen,
  The dusky Ethiop queen
Smiled on King Solomon.

3

Wisest of men, he knew
  The languages of all
  The creatures great or small
That trod the earth or flew.

4

Across an ant-hill led
  The king's path, and he heard
  Its small folk, and their word
He thus interpreted:

By permission of Houghton Mifflin Company.

5

"Here comes the king men greet
  As wise and good and just,
  To crush us in the dust
Under his heedless feet."

6

The great king bowed his head,
  And saw the wide surprise
  Of the Queen of Sheba's eyes
As he told her what they said.

7

"Oh, King," she whispered sweet,
  "Too happy fate have they
  Who perish in thy way,
Beneath thy gracious feet!

8

"Thou of the God-lent crown,
  Shall these vile creatures dare
  Murmur against thee where
The knees of kings kneel down?"

9

"Nay," Solomon replied,
  "The wise and strong should seek
  The welfare of the weak";
And turned his horse aside.

10

His train, with quick alarm,
  Curved with their leader round
  The ant-hill's peopled mound,
And left it free from harm.

11

The jeweled head bent low;
  "O king!" she said, "henceforth
  The secret of thy worth
And wisdom well I know.

12

"Happy must be the state
  Whose ruler heedeth more
  The murmurs of the poor
Than flatteries of the great."
—John Greenleaf Whittier.

THE DESTRUCTION OF SENNACHERIB

Perhaps no other poem of Lord Byron's is so popular with young readers as this splendid oriental picture of the siege of Jerusalem and the destruction of the hosts of the Assyrian king. Sennacherib was in some respects the most interesting of Assyrian monarchs and a typical representative of oriental haughtiness, violence, and power. He was king of Assyria for twenty-four years

—from B. C. 705 to 681. At the time of the event described in the poem, Hezekiah was king of Judah, and had as his temporary ally the king of Egypt. Sennacherib, after defeating the Egyptian force before Ekron, took the city, put to death the priests and chief men, hung up their bodies on stakes all around the city, and turned his attention to Jerusalem. In one of the royal inscriptions in Nineveh, discovered among the ruins of the palace, the great king Sennacherib gives this account of his expedition against Hezekiah:

> I took forty-six of his strong fenced cities; and of the smaller towns which were scattered about, and plundered a countless number. And from these places I captured and carried off as spoils 200,150 people, old and young, male and female, together with horses and mares, asses and camels, oxen and sheep, a countless multitude. And Hezekiah himself I shut up in Jerusalem, his capital city, like a bird in a cage, building towers around the city to hem him in, and raising banks of earth against the gates, so as to prevent his escape.

He then tells how Hezekiah, after giving up the treasures of the temple and the palace, came to the conclusion that further resistance would be in vain, and offered to surrender.

Here Sennacherib's account ends, but we know from the Scriptures and from Egyptian history that there is more to be told. Sennacherib demanded unconditional surrender of Jerusalem, and sent three officers to make the demand. While they were negotiating and boasting outside the city walls, Hezekiah received a message from God, through Isaiah, according to the

THE DESTRUCTION OF SENNACHERIB 93

Biblical account, that he would "put his hook in Sennacherib's nose and his bridle in his lips and turn him back by the way by which he came. . . . He shall not come into the city nor shoot an arrow there." The campaign now took a new turn. What happened that night, probably due to a plague resulting from utter neglect of sanitation, is told in *Second Kings* in these words:

35. And it came to pass that night, that the angel of the Lord went out, and smote in the camp of the Assyrians an hundred, fourscore and five thousand: and when they arose early in the morning, behold, they *were* all dead corpses.

36. So Sennacherib king of Assyria departed, and went and returned, and dwelt at Nineveh.

There is no more dramatic record in ancient history than this. Details of it may be found in Rawlinson's *Ancient Monarchies, Volume II.,* and in *Second Kings 18:13-37,* and *Isaiah 36* and *37.*

A foot-note in Rawlinson says:

I cannot accept the view that the Assyrian army was destroyed by the simoon, owing to the foreign forces of Sennacherib being little acquainted with the means of avoiding this unusual enemy. The simoon would not have destroyed one army and left the other unhurt. The narrative implies a secret, sudden taking away of life during sleep, by divine interposition.

These historical facts will assist the understanding, but the imagination must be used to call up the scenes so vividly portrayed in the poem. Every line should be carefully studied. Notice the contrast, as set forth in the second stanza, between the state of the Assyrian army before and after the pestilence swept over it.

THE DESTRUCTION OF SENNACHERIB

1

The Assyrian came down like the wolf on the fold,
And his cohorts were gleaming in purple and gold;
And the sheen of their spears was like stars on the sea,
When the blue wave rolls nightly on deep Galilee.

2

Like the leaves of the forest when summer is green,
That host with their banners at sunset were seen;
Like the leaves of the forest when Autumn hath blown,
That host on the morrow lay withered and strown.

3

For the Angel of Death spread his wings on the blast,
And breathed in the face of the foe as he passed;
And the eyes of the sleepers waxed deadly and chill,
And their hearts but once heaved, and forever grew still!

4

And there lay the steed with his nostrils all wide,
But through it there rolled not the breath of his pride;
And the foam of his gasping lay white on the turf,
And cold as the spray of the rock-beating surf.

5

And there lay the rider distorted and pale,
With the dew on his brow and the rust on his mail;
And the tents were all silent, the banners alone,
The lances unlifted, the trumpets unblown.

6

And the widows of Ashur are loud in their wail,
And their idols are broke in the temple of Baal;
And the might of the Gentile, unsmote by the sword,
Hath melted like snow in the glance of the Lord.

—George Gordon Byron.

The Angel of Death—the pestilence.
Ashur—another name for Assyria.
Baal—one of the chief gods of Assyria.*
The Gentile—King Sennacherib.
Glance of the Lord—the pestilence.

* The story of how the idols were broken in the house of Baal is told in a most interesting way in *Second Kings 10:18-29:*

And Jehu gathered all the people together, and said unto them, Ahab served Baal a little; *but* Jehu shall serve him much.

Now therefore call unto me all the prophets of Baal, all his servants, and all his priests; let none be wanting: for I have a great sacrifice *to do* to Baal; whosoever shall be wanting, he shall not live. But Jehu did *it* in subtilty, to the intent that he might destroy the worshippers of Baal.

And Jehu said, Proclaim a solemn assembly for Baal. And they proclaimed *it*.

And Jehu sent through all Israel: and all the worshippers of Baal came, so that there was not a man left that came not. And they came into the house of Baal; and the house of Baal was full from one end to another.

And he said unto him that *was* over the vestry, Bring forth vestments for all the worshippers of Baal. And he brought them forth vestments.

And Jehu went, and Jehonadab the son of Rechab, into the house of Baal, and said unto the worshippers of Baal, Search, and look that there be here with you none of the servants of the LORD, but the worshippers of Baal only.

And when they went in to offer sacrifices and burnt offerings, Jehu appointed four-score men without, and said, *If* any of the men whom I have brought into your hands escape, *he that letteth him go,* his life *shall be* for the life of him.

And it came to pass, as soon as he had made an end of offering the burnt offering, that Jehu said to the guard and to the captains, Go in, *and* slay them; let none come forth. And they smote them with the edge of the sword; and the guard and the captains cast *them* out, and went to the city of the house of Baal.

And they brought forth the images out of the house of Baal, and burned them.

And they brake down the image of Baal, and brake down the house of Baal, and made it a draught house unto this day.

Thus Jehu destroyed Baal out of Israel.

ROBIN HOOD

Robin Hood, the English outlaw, is said to have lived in the twelfth century. According to popular account, he and his followers inhabited Sherwood Forest in Nottinghamshire, and also the woodlands of Barnsdale in the adjoining West Riding. He supported himself by levying tolls on the wealthy, especially on ecclesiastics, and by hunting the deer. The principal members of his band were his lieutenant Little John, his chaplain Friar Tuck, William Deadlock, George-a-Greene, Muck, the miller's son, Allan-a-Dale, and Maid Marian. His skill with the longbow and quarterstaff was celebrated in tradition. What basis of fact there is for the story of Robin Hood is doubtful, and there are various theories as to his historical identity.

The poem is a graceful description of the old free and happy days in Sherwood Forest, when men did not have to worry about rents and leases.

ROBIN HOOD

1

No! those days are gone away
And their hours are old and gray,
And their minutes buried all
Under the downtrodden pall
Of the leaves of many years;
Many times have Winter's shears,
Frozen North, and chilling East,
Sounded tempests to the feast
Of the forest's whispering fleeces
Since men knew no rents nor leases.

2

No! the bugle sounds no more,
And the twanging bow no more;
Silent is the ivory shrill,
Past the heath and up the hill;
There is no mid-forest laugh,
Whose lone echo gives the half
To some wight amazed to hear
Jesting, deep in forest drear.

3

On the fairest time of June
You may go, with sun or moon,
Or the seven stars to light you,
Or the polar ray to right you;
But you never may behold
Little John, or Robin bold—
Never one, of all the clan
Thrumming on an empty can
Some old hunting ditty, while
He doth his green way beguile
To fair hostess Merriment
Down beside the pasture Trent;
For he left the merry tale,
Messenger for spicy ale.

4

Gone the merry morris din;
Gone the song of Gamelyn;
Gone the tough-belted outlaw
Idling in the "greenè shawe"—
All are gone away and past;
And if Robin should be cast
Sudden from his tufted grave,
And if Marian should have
Once again her forest days,
She would weep, and he would craze;
He would swear, for all his oaks,
Fallen beneath the dockyard strokes

Have rotted on the briny seas;
She would weep that her wild bees
Sang not to her—Strange! that honey
Can't be got without hard money!

5

So it is! you let us sing
Honor to the old bow string!
Honor to the bugle-horn!
Honor to the woods unshorn!
Honor to the Lincoln green!
Honor to the archer keen!
Honor to tight Little John,
And the horse he rode upon!
Honor to bold Robin Hood,
Sleeping in the underwood!
Honor to Maid Marian
And to all the Sherwood clan!
Though their days have hurried by,
Let us two a burden try!

—John Keats.

Greenè shawe—a green grove.
Lincoln green—a color of cloth formerly made in England.
Whispering fleeces—leaves of the forest.
Ivory shrill—a whistle or fife.
Wight—man.
Pasture Trent—a field by the Trent river.
Morris—a kind of dance.
Gamelyn—one of the foresters who became "king of the outlaws," according to tradition.

Burden—a refrain.

In Shakespeare's *As You Like It* occurs this little forest song:

> Under the greenwood tree
> Who loves to lie with me,
> And turn his merry note
> Unto the sweet bird's throat,
> Come hither, come hither, come hither;
> Here shall he see
> No enemy,
> But winter and rough weather.

Robin Hood figures prominently in Scott's novel, *Ivanhoe,* and in many a song and tale.

THE NIGHT BEFORE WATERLOO

From "Childe Harold's Pilgrimage"

In *Vanity Fair,* chapter 29, Thackeray says:

"There never was, since the days of Darius, such a brilliant train of camp-followers as hung round the train of the Duke of Wellington's army in the Low Countries, in 1815, and led it dancing and feasting, as it were, up to the very brink of battle. A certain ball which a noble duchess gave at Brussels on the 15th of June in the above-named year is historical. All Brussels had been in a state of excitement about it, and I have heard from ladies who were in that town at the period, that the talk and interest of persons of their own sex regarding the ball was much greater even than in respect of the enemy in their front."

The ball was given by the Duchess of Richmond, in honor of the officers of the English and allied armies. In her *Personal Recollections* Lady de Ros, a daughter of the Duchess of Richmond, says:

"When the Duke of Wellington arrived, rather late, at the ball, I was dancing, but at once went up to him to ask about the rumors (of battle). He said very gravely, 'Yes. They are true; we are off to-morrow.' This terrible news was circulated directly, and while some of the officers hurried away, others remained at the ball, and actually had not time to change their clothes, but fought in evening costume.

"I went with my oldest brother . . . to his house, which stood in our garden, to help him pack up, after which we returned to the ball-room, where we found some energetic and heartless ladies still dancing. . . . It was a dreadful evening, taking leave of friends and acquaintances, many never to be seen again. . . . The Duke of Brunswick, as he took leave of me in the ante-room adjoining the ball-room, made me a civil speech as to the Brunswickers being sure to distinguish themselves. . . . I remember being quite provoked at Lord Hay . . . for his delight at the idea of going into action; and the first news we had on the 16th was that he and the Duke of Brunswick were killed. . . . At the ball supper I sat next to the Duke of Wellington. In the course of the evening the Duke asked my father for a map of the country. He put his finger on Waterloo, saying the battle would be fought there."

The battle which occurred the next day is known as the battle of Quatre Bras; forty-eight hours later came the great battle of Waterloo, when Napoleon was defeated by the allied forces of Europe under the Duke of Wellington.

WATERLOO

1

There was a sound of revelry by night,
    And Belgium's capital had gathered then
Her beauty and her chivalry, and bright
    The lamps shone o'er fair women and brave men;
    A thousand hearts beat happily; and when
Music arose with its voluptuous swell,
    Soft eyes looked love to eyes which spake again,
And all went merry as a marriage-bell:
But hush! hark! a deep sound strikes like a rising knell!

2

Did ye not hear it? No; 'twas but the wind,
    Or the car rattling o'er the stony street.
On with the dance! let joy be unconfined!
    No sleep till morn, when Youth and Pleasure meet
    To chase the glowing Hours with flying feet!
But hark!—that heavy sound breaks in once more,
    As if the clouds its echo would repeat;

And nearer, clearer, deadlier, than before!
Arm! arm! it is—it is—the cannon's opening roar!

3

Within a windowed niche of that high hall
  Sate Brunswick's fated chieftain; he did hear
That sound the first amidst the festival,
  And caught its tone with Death's prophetic ear;
  And when they smiled because he deemed it near,
His heart more truly knew that peal too well
  Which stretched his father on a bloody bier,
And roused the vengeance blood alone could quell;
He rushed into the field, and, foremost fighting, fell.

4

Ah! then and there was hurrying to and fro,
  And gathering tears, and tremblings of distress,
And cheeks all pale which but an hour ago
  Blushed at the praise of their own loveliness.
  And there were sudden partings, such as press
The life from out young hearts, and choking sighs
  Which ne'er might be repeated; who would guess
If ever more should meet those mutual eyes,
Since upon night so sweet such awful morn could rise!

5

And there was mounting in hot haste; the steed,
  The mustering squadron, and the clattering car

Went pouring forward with impetuous speed,
  And swiftly forming in the ranks of war;
  And the deep thunder peal on peal afar;
And near, the beat of the alarming drum
  Roused up the soldier ere the morning star;
While thronged the citizens with terror dumb,
Or whispering with white lips, "The foe! They come!
    They come!"

*   *   *   *   *   *   *

6

Last noon beheld them full of lusty life,
  Last eve in beauty's circle proudly gay;
The midnight brought the signal sound of strife,
  The morn, the marshalling in arms; the day,
  Battle's magnificently stern array!
The thunderclouds close o'er it, which when rent
  The earth is covered thick with other clay,
Which her own clay shall cover, heaped and pent,
Rider and horse, friend, foe, in one red burial blent!

—George Gordon Byron.

Car—a two-wheeled vehicle.

Brunswick's fated chieftain—The Duke of Brunswick was killed in the battle next day. His Father, Duke Ferdinand, had been killed by the French at Jena in 1806. (Stanza three.)

Clay—soldiers, men; referring to the Biblical statement that "God formed man of the dust of the ground."

THE CHAMBERED NAUTILUS

The chambered nautilus is a small shellfish found in the South Pacific and Indian oceans and the Mediterranean Sea, especially about Sicily. A large and perfect shell will weigh six or seven ounces. The exterior crust of the shell is whitish, with fawn-colored streaks and bands, and the interior has a beautiful pearly lustre. The shell is coiled in a flat spiral, much like the shell of a snail, and the interior is divided by partitions into numerous chambers, each succeeding chamber being larger than the last. The animal lives in a very small chamber at first, and every time it moves into another it builds a partition between, until a certain stage is reached in the growth of the animal, when no new chambers are formed.

Running through the center of the shell and connecting the chambers one with another, the first with the last, is a small cord. Even so the cord of memory connects us with the house of our childhood, no matter how small and humble it may have been, and no matter how great the difference or the distance between it and one's present home.

With this simple information, Dr. Holmes's familiar and beautiful poem is easily understood. It will be much better, of course, if the reader have a nautilus shell so that he may see its "chambered cells," its "sunless crypts," its "irised ceiling," its "idle doors."

It is well to conceive of the author with a broken nautilus shell lying before him as he wrote the verses about it.

THE CHAMBERED NAUTILUS

1

This is the ship of pearl, which, poets feign,
    Sails the unshadowed main,—
    The venturous bark that flings
On the sweet summer wind its purpled wings
In gulfs enchanted, where the Siren sings,
    And coral reefs lie bare,
Where the cold sea-maids rise to sun their streaming hair.

2

Its webs of living gauze no more unfurl;
    Wrecked is the ship of pearl!
    And every chambered cell
Where its dim dreaming life was wont to dwell,
As the frail tenant shaped his growing shell,
    Before thee lies revealed,—
Its irised ceiling rent, its sunless crypt unsealed!

3

Year after year beheld the silent toil
    That spread his lustrous coil;
    Still, as the spiral grew,
He left the past year's dwelling for the new,

Stole with soft steps its shining archway through,
  Built up its idle door,
Stretched in his last-found home, and knew the old no
    more.

4

Thanks for the heavenly message brought by thee,
  Child of the wandering sea,
  Cast from her lap, forlorn!
From thy dead lips a clearer note is born
Than ever Triton blew from wreathèd horn!
  While on mine ear it rings,
Through the deep caves of thought I hear a voice that
    sings:—

5

Build thee more stately mansions, O my soul,
  As the swift seasons roll!
  Leave thy low-vaulted past!
Let each new temple, nobler than the last,
Shut thee from heaven with a dome more vast,
  Till thou at length art free,
Leaving thine outgrown shell by life's unresting sea!

—Oliver Wendell Holmes.

The *ship of pearl* is, of course, the shell itself.
Unshadowed main—ocean.
Purpled wings are gauze-like projections which the animal was popularly supposed to have the power of throwing out in the manner of sails.

Sirens, in mythology, were birds with faces of women, found on the shores of the Mediterranean, who by their sweet voices enticed to the shores those who were sailing by, and then killed them.

Wrecked is the ship of pearl—the broken shell.

Crypt—cell or chamber where the animal lived.

Dead lips—the empty shell.

Triton—the trumpeter of Neptune, the chief god of the sea.

Dome more vast—a loftier and more spacious chamber.

The chief emotion aroused by the poem is aspiration; and this is its chief meaning. The final stanza expresses it in a beautiful and effective way.

WOLSEY'S FAREWELL TO CROMWELL

From "King Henry VIII," Act iii, Scene 2.

The supposed address of Cardinal Wolsey to Thomas Cromwell, his successor in the king's favor, is better understood when one knows the facts of Wolsey's career. He was born in Suffolk, England, 1471, educated at Oxford, and became chaplain to Henry VIII. By his devoted and brilliant service he soon rose to high favor at court. Henry VIII. made him Archbishop of York in 1514, Lord Chancellor of England in 1515, and gave him almost unlimited power. The Pope created him a cardinal, and he acted as if he were really one of the sovereigns of Europe. His ambition was to become Pope, and twice he almost succeeded. His rise and influence lay in his willingness to serve the king at all times.

Cavendish, who acted as his servant and wrote his life, tells us that he lived in splendid style. In his household, waiting upon him, holding various offices, were many lords and gentlemen, and under them innumerable servants, clerks of the kitchen, yeoman of the scullery, yeoman of his chariot and his stirrup, cup-bearers, carvers, and grooms. The head cook "went daily in velvet or in satin, with a chain of gold." He had doctors, chaplains, choristers innumerable, the list filling two or three pages of Cavendish's book. "When he went out in the morning his cardinal's hat was borne by some gentleman of worship right solemnly," also two great crosses. Then the gentlemen ushers going before him, bareheaded, cried aloud, "On before my lord and master, on before and make way for my lord the cardinal." Thus he went down through the hall, the sergeant-at-arms before him carrying a great mace of silver, and two gentlemen carrying two great pillars of silver. And when he came to the hall-door, there stood his mule caparisoned in crimson velvet, with saddle of same, with gilt stirrups. When he was mounted there were in attendance upon him two cross-bearers and pillar-bearers, each upon a great horse, each in fine scarlet. Then he marched forward with a train of gentlemen, and gentlemen with four footmen, each bearing a gilt pole-axe in his hand. "And thus passed he forth until he came to Westminster hall door." His houses, or palaces, were fit for a king; one at Hampton Court, the other at Whitehall. They were filled with magnificent furniture, costly furnishings, beds of silk, arras, gold and silver plate, and tapestry in profusion. This gives us an idea of his splendor. Notwithstanding all this display, it is said he judged every estate according to its merits and deserts, sparing neither high nor low. Nor did he forget his old home, nor the university, nor the good education that had helped him to rise; with true generosity he founded a college at Oxford called Cardinal College, afterward renamed Christ Church College.

Had Wolsey ever seen that part of the Catholic service when, as the fire consumes sumptuous apparel, the choristers sing, *"sic transit gloria mundi"* (so passes away the glory of the world)? The time was drawing near when his glory would pass away.

The king turned against him because he was not able to bring about a divorce from Queen Catherine. The king wished to marry Anne Boleyn. At last Anne Boleyn demanded and obtained from the king Wolsey's dismissal in disgrace.

Cavendish says that he gave up to the king all of his riches, gold and silver plate, velvet, cloth of silver, cloth of gold, satin damask, tapestry and tufted taffeta. Then a sad parting took place between him and his servants as he broke up his great household, when he said farewell to his many servants, to whom he had been so kind and generous. Cavendish says, "Beholding this goodly number of his servants, he could not speak to them until the tears ran down his cheeks, which few tears seen by his servants caused the fountains of water to gush out of their faithful eyes in such sort as would cause a cruel heart to lament."

Soon after this he was sent to his archbishopric of York, and the king selected as his own advisers Sir Thomas More and Thomas Cromwell.

Soon Wolsey was charged with high treason and summoned to London. His proud heart was broken, and when he reached Leicester Abbey he was so ill he could hardly sit upon his mule, and he died a few days later. As he lay dying and looked back over his strange life, through all his ambition and industry, his power and his splendor, he said, "If I had served my God as diligently as I have served my king, he would not have given me over in my gray hairs."

This historical sketch will help to an understanding of such passages as these:

"Wolsey, that once trod the ways of glory."

"Mark but my fall, and that that ruined me.
Cromwell, I charge thee, fling away ambition."

"O Cromwell, Cromwell,
Had I but served my God with half the zeal
I served my king, He would not in mine age
Have left me naked to mine enemies."

It is an interesting fact that Cromwell did not profit by Wolsey's experience. After rising from the state of a blacksmith's son to be Lord Chancellor of England, and almost as powerful as Wolsey had been, he at last came under King Henry's displeasure, and was executed, 1540, without the privilege of defending himself. He himself had introduced the law that persons accused of high treason against the king should not be heard in their own behalf. By a remarkable retribution he was the first to suffer under that law.

WOLSEY'S FAREWELL TO CROMWELL

Cromwell, I did not think to shed a tear
In all my miseries; but thou hast forced me,
Out of thy honest truth, to play the woman.
Let's dry our eyes; and thus far hear me, Cromwell;
And,—when I am forgotten, as I shall be,
And sleep in dull cold marble, where no mention
Of me more must be heard of,—say, I taught thee;
Say Wolsey—that once trod the ways of glory,
And sounded all the depths and shoals of honor—
Found thee a way, out of his wreck, to rise in,
A sure and safe one, though thy master missed it.
Mark but my fall, and that that ruined me:
Cromwell, I charge thee, fling away ambition;
By that sin fell the angels; how can man, then,
The image of his Maker, hope to win by 't?

Love thyself last; cherish those hearts that hate
 thee;
Corruption wins not more than honesty.
Still in thy right hand carry gentle peace,
To silence envious tongues. Be just, and fear not.
Let all the ends thou aim'st at be thy country's,
Thy God's, and truth's; then if thou fall'st, O
 Cromwell,
Thou fall'st a blessed martyr. Serve the king;
And,—Prithee, lead me in:
There take an inventory of all I have,
To the last penny; 'tis the king's: my robe,
And my integrity to heaven, is all
I dare now call mine own. O Cromwell, Cromwell,
Had I but served my God with half the zeal
I served my king, He would not in mine age
Have left me naked to mine enemies.

—William Shakespeare.

THE RAINY DAY

The Rainy Day is a little poem perfect in form and true in its interpretation of life. Notice in the first stanza the picture of a vine clinging to an old gray stone wall; it is the fall of the year, the wind is blowing through the cold rain, and the leaves are falling from the vine. If the reader is familiar with any such scene as this he should be led to tell about it before passing on to the reading of the next stanza. He cannot understand the rest of the poem unless he knows or can imagine what an old vine-covered wall is like in the fall of the year when the leaves turn yellow and brown, and the wind and rains scatter them over the ground.

In the second stanza the facts of nature pictured in the first stanza are applied to life. Thoughts are the vines, the past years are the old gray wall, and the hopes of youth are the dead leaves that fall thick in the blast. The wind and the rain are the sorrows and the griefs of life.

Notice that stanza one interprets stanza two, line for line; for example, compare the third line of the first stanza with the third line of the second, and the fourth line of the first with the fourth line of the second.

THE RAINY DAY

1

The day is cold, and dark, and dreary;
It rains, and the wind is never weary;
The vine still clings to the moldering **wall,**
But at every gust the dead leaves fall,
   And the day is dark and dreary.

2

My life is cold, and dark, and dreary;
It rains, and the wind is never weary;
My thoughts still cling to the moldering **Past,**
But the hopes of youth fall thick in the blast,
   And the days are dark and dreary.

3

Be still, sad heart! and cease repining;
Behind the clouds is the sun still shining;
Thy fate is the common fate of all,
Into each life some rain must fall,
　Some days must be dark and dreary.
　　　　　　—Henry Wadsworth Longfellow.

The reader's attention is called to Dr. Boone's discussion of this poem in the Introduction to this book.

IN AN AGE OF FOPS AND TOYS

This is a part of a poem on slavery, called *Voluntaries*. "To hazard all in Freedom's fight" has, therefore, a definite application and meaning. History shows that a great multitude of "heroic boys," both North and South, heard Duty whisper low, *Thou must,* and answered with their lives, *I can.*

IN AN AGE OF FOPS AND TOYS

In an age of fops and toys,
　Wanting wisdom, void of right,
Who shall nerve heroic boys
　To hazard all in Freedom's fight,—
Break sharply off their jolly games,
　Forsake their comrades gay

By permission of Houghton Mifflin Company.

>   And quit proud homes and youthful dames
>   For famine, toil and fray?
>   Yet on the nimble air benign
>   Speed nimbler messages,
>   That waft the breath of grace divine
>   To hearts in sloth and ease.
>   So nigh is grandeur to our dust,
>   So near is God to man,
>   When Duty whispers low, *Thou must,*
>   The youth replies, *I can.*
>   —Ralph Waldo Emerson.

O CAPTAIN! MY CAPTAIN!

This remarkably fine poem will mean almost nothing to the young reader unless some explanation is given. Its author was a volunteer nurse in the army hospitals at Washington during the Civil War. He knew and loved Lincoln, the great president, and this poem is a tribute to him. It is filled with two emotions—the feeling of patriotic joy over the results of the war, and the feeling of personal grief for the death of Lincoln.

In this poem he conceives of the nation as a ship. This ship has been on a fearful trip—the Civil War. He conceives of Lincoln as the captain of the ship. The fearful trip has been successful, and the shores are crowded with rejoicing throngs to welcome it home, but just as the port is reached the captain (Lincoln) falls dead on the deck. Of course this refers to his assassination at the close of the war.

In the last stanza he calls Lincoln "father" because of his love for him. For the same reason he calls him "My captain."

Thousands who knew the great president and hundreds of thousands who did not know him have, with Whitman, "walked the deck (where) my Captain lies, fallen cold and dead."

This is a good poem for the class to read immediately after they have studied about the Civil War and the death of Lincoln.

They must use their imagination and try to see the awful picture as Whitman draws it, and perhaps they may be able to experience some of the patriotic emotions of its author.

O CAPTAIN! MY CAPTAIN!

1

O Captain! my Captain; our fearful trip is done;
The ship has weather'd every rack, the prize we sought
    is won;
The port is near, the bells I hear, the people all exulting,
While follow eyes the steady keel, the vessel grim and
    daring:
      But O heart! heart! heart!
        O the bleeding drops of red,
      Where on the deck my Captain lies,
        Fallen cold and dead.

2

O Captain! my Captain! rise up and hear the bells;
Rise up—for you the flag is flung—for you the bugle trills;
For you bouquets and ribbon'd wreaths, for you the shores a-crowding,
For you they call, the swaying mass, their eager faces turning;
  Here, Captain, dear father;
    This arm beneath your head;
   It is some dream that on the deck,
    You've fallen cold and dead.

3

My Captain does not answer, his lips are pale and still;
My father does not feel my arm, he has no pulse nor will;
The ship is anchored safe and sound, its voyage closed and done,
From fearful trip the victor ship comes in with object won;
  Exult, O shores, and ring, O bells!
   But I, with mournful tread,
  Walk the deck my Captain lies,
    Fallen cold and dead.

—Walt Whitman.

The prize we sought—the preservation of the Union.
Weathered every rack—weathered every storm.

Follow eyes the steady keel—still anxious for her safe arrival in port.

The first four lines of the second stanza present a splendid picture of national rejoicing.

The closing lines of Longfellow's *Building of the Ship* should be read in this connection:

> Thou, too, sail on, O Ship of State!
> Sail on, O UNION, strong and great!
> Humanity, with all its fears,
> With all the hopes of future years,
> Is hanging breathless on thy fate!
> We know what Master laid thy keel,
> What Workmen wrought thy ribs of steel,
> Who made each mast, and sail, and rope,
> What anvils rang, what hammers beat,
> In what a forge and what a heat
> Were shaped the anchors of thy hope!
>
> Fear not each sudden sound and shock.
> 'T is of the wave, and not the rock;
> 'T is but the flapping of the sail,
> And not a rent made by the gale!
> In spite of rock and tempest's roar,
> In spite of false lights on the shore,
> Sail on, nor fear to breast the sea!
> Our hearts, our hopes, are all with thee:
> Our hearts, our hopes, our prayers, our **tears,**
> Our faith triumphant o'er our fears,
> Are all with thee,—are all with thee!

ALADDIN

The *Arabian Nights,* sometimes called *The Thousand and One Nights,* is one of the most widely read collections of tales ever written. The statement has been made that it has been read more widely than almost any other production of the human mind. They are wild and fanciful oriental stories, first collected and written down about the end of the fifteenth century, but nobody knows who was the author. They are supposed to have originated in Egypt.

One of the characters in the *Arabian Nights* is Aladdin, a poor boy, who becomes possessed of a wonderful lamp. When he rubs this lamp, genii appear around him and offer to do his bidding, to get for him whatever he may like. One object to which he takes a fancy is the sultan's daughter, and even this prize is won for him by the slaves of his wonderful lamp. The sultan lets him know that if he will send the sultan forty baskets of diamonds carried by forty black slaves, and each black slave led by a white slave, he may have his daughter to be his wife. Aladdin rubs his lamp, the genii appear, he tells them his desire, and, behold, the thing is done. Aladdin builds a marvelous palace, and the lamp is hung up somewhere in a corner, nobody but Aladdin being aware of its value. By and by the old wizard, from whom Aladdin had obtained the lamp by accident, comes along, disguised as a peddler, and offers to trade some new silver lamps for the old lamp. The servants in the palace trade the old lamp for the new silver ones.

This is but a small part of the story of Aladdin's lamp, but it may serve to explain this poem.

ALADDIN

1

When I was a beggarly boy,
    And lived in a cellar damp,
I had not a friend nor a toy,
    But I had Aladdin's lamp;
When I could not sleep for the cold,
    I had fire enough in my brain,
And builded, with roofs of gold,
    My beautiful castles in Spain.

2

Since then I have toiled day and night,
    I have money and power, good store,
But I'd give all my lamps of silver bright
    For the one that is mine no more;
Take, Fortune, whatever you choose;
    You gave, and may snatch again:
I have nothing 't would pain me to lose,
    For I own no more castles in Spain!

—James Russell Lowell.

Aladdin's lamp—the imagination, by which we fancy we have the good and the beautiful things of the world, no matter how poor we may be.

Castles in Spain—castles in the air, or existing only in our imaginations, but which may be very real to us and very wonderful and very beautiful. The youth who builds "castles in Spain" is dreaming his dreams and seeing his visions; and without them no great thing is accomplished.

I had not a friend nor a toy—There are thousands of children, even today, who never have any toys. This is one of the saddest fates of childhood.

I had fire enough in my brain—the fire of imagination and fancy.

Good store—plenty.

But I'd give all my lamps of silver bright—This has reference to the trading by the old wizard in the tale, of his new silver lamps for Aladdin's lamp.

The second stanza means that youth has passed away and success has been attained, but the visions and pictures and dreams of boyhood are no more. He has lost Aladdin's lamp.

Fortune, in the last stanza, is the old wizard from whom Aladdin got the lamp and who took it from him again.

Read *The Arabian Nights.*

THE OLD CLOCK ON THE STAIRS

An introductory note to this poem in Houghton, Mifflin & Company's admirable eleven-volume edition of Longfellow's works states that the house referred to is now known as the Plunkett mansion, in Pittsfield, Massachusetts, the homestead of Mrs. Longfellow's maternal grandfather, whither Longfellow went after his marriage in the summer of 1843.

The same authority explains the origin of the poem and the significance of the refrain:

>Forever—never!
>Never—forever!

Under date of November 12, 1845, Longfellow wrote in his diary:

"Began a poem on a clock, with the words 'Forever, never,' as the burden, suggested by the words of Bridaine, the old French missionary, who said of eternity: 'It is a clock whose pendulum says and repeats without ceasing only these two words in the silence of the tombs, Forever, never! Never, forever! And during these terrible revolutions a miserable soul cries out, What time is it? And another unhappy one answers him, Eternity.'"

The meaning is made clear in the last stanza of the poem, which says:

> Never here, forever there,
> Where all parting, pain, and care,
> And death, and time shall disappear,—
> Forever there, but never here!

THE OLD CLOCK ON THE STAIRS

1

Somewhat back from the village street
Stands the old-fashioned country-seat.
Across its antique portico
Tall poplar trees their shadows throw;
And from its station in the hall
An ancient timepiece says to all,—
    "Forever—never!
    Never—forever!"

2

Half-way up the stairs it stands,
And points and beckons with its hands
From its case of massive oak,
Like a monk, who, under his cloak,
Crosses himself, and sighs, alas!
With sorrowful voice to all who pass,—
    "Forever—never!
    Never—forever!"

3

By day its voice is low and light;
But in the silent dead of night,
Distinct as a passing footstep's fall,
It echoes along the vacant hall,
Along the ceiling, along the floor,
And seems to say, at each chamber-door,—
    "Forever—never!
    Never—forever!"

4

Through days of sorrow and of mirth,
Through days of death and days of birth,
Through every swift vicissitude
Of changeful time, unchanged it has stood,
And as if, like God, it all things saw,
It calmly repeats those words of awe,—
    "Forever—never!
    Never—forever!"

5

In that mansion used to be
Free-hearted Hospitality;
His great fires up the chimney roared;
The stranger feasted at his board;
But, like the skeleton at the feast,
That warning timepiece never ceased,—
    "Forever—never!
      Never—forever!"

6

There groups of merry children played,
There youths and maidens dreaming strayed;
O precious hours! O golden prime,
And affluence of love and time!
Even as a miser counts his gold,
Those hours the ancient timepiece told,—
    "Forever—never!
      Never—forever!"

7

From that chamber, clothed in white,
The bride came forth on her wedding night;
There, in that silent room below,
The dead lay in his shroud of snow;
And in the hush that followed the prayer,
Was heard the old clock on the stair,—
    "Forever—never!
      Never—forever!"

8

All are scattered now and fled,
Some are married, some are dead;
And when I ask, with throbs of pain,
"Ah! when shall they all meet again?"
As in the days long since gone by,
The ancient timepiece makes reply,—
    "Forever—never!
    Never—forever!"

9

Never here, forever there,
Where all parting, pain, and care,
And death, and time shall disappear,—
Forever there, but never here!
The horologe of Eternity
Sayeth this incessantly,—
    "Forever—never!
    Never—forever!"
      —Henry Wadsworth Longfellow.

THE FOUR WINDS

The Four Winds has no hidden meaning, but to read it with the understanding is difficult. It contains twenty-six distinct mental images—the first stanza has

six, the second seven, the third six and the last seven.
To see them all clearly as one reads the lines is not
easy to do, but it must be done if the poem is to give
the reader its full value. The meaning of the poem is
revealed in the last line. It is a good piece with which
to test one's imaginative power—and the imagination
is the chief agent in good reading, whether silent or oral.

THE FOUR WINDS

1

Wind of the North,
Wind of the Norland snows,
Wind of the winnowed skies and sharp, clear stars—
Blow cold and keen across the naked hills,
And crisp the lowland pools with crystal films,
And blur the casement squares with glittering ice,
But go not near my love.

2

Wind of the West,
Wind of the few, far clouds,
Wind of the gold and crimson sunset lands—
Blow fresh and pure across the peaks and plains,
And broaden the blue spaces of the heavens,
And sway the grasses and the mountain pines,
But let my dear one rest.

From *The Dead Nymph and Other Poems*
Copyright, 1891, By Charles Scribner's Sons

3

Wind of the East,
Wind of the sunrise seas,
Wind of the clinging mists and gray, harsh rains—
Blow moist and chill across the wastes of brine,
And shut the sun out, and the moon and stars,
And lash the boughs against the dripping eaves,
Yet keep thou from my love.
But thou, sweet Wind!

4

Wind of the South,
Wind from the bowers of jasmine and of rose—
Over magnolia blooms and lilied lakes
And flowering forests come with dewy wings,
And stir the petals at her feet, and kiss
The low mound where she lies.

—Charles Henry Lüders.

THE BIRDS OF KILLINGWORTH

Killingworth is a village in Connecticut. An old resident of the place is quoted (in the Houghton, Mifflin & Company edition of Longfellow's works) as saying that the men of Killingworth

"did yearly, in the spring, choose two leaders and then the two sides were formed [to see who could kill the most birds]. Their special game was the hawk, the owl, the crow, and the blackbird, and any other bird supposed to be mischievous to the corn. Some years each side would bring them in by the bushel. This was followed up for only a few years, for the birds began to grow scarce."

Longfellow's poem is doubtless based upon this incident.

THE BIRDS OF KILLINGWORTH

1

It was the season when through all the land
  The merle and mavis build, and building sing
Those lovely lyrics, written by His hand,
  Whom Saxon Cædmon calls the Blithe-heart King;
When on the boughs the purple buds expand,
  The banners of the vanguard of the Spring,
And rivulets, rejoicing, rush and leap,
And wave their fluttering signals from the steep.

2

The robin and the bluebird, piping loud,
  Filled all the blossoming orchards with their glee;
The sparrows chirped as if they still were proud
  Their race in Holy Writ should mentioned be;
And hungry crows assembled in a crowd,
  Clamored their piteous prayer incessantly,
Knowing who hears the ravens cry, and said:
"Give us, O Lord, this day, our daily bread!"

3

Across the Sound the birds of passage sailed,
  Speaking some unknown language strange and sweet
Of tropic isle remote, and passing hailed
  The village with the cheers of all their fleet;
Or quarrelling together, laughed and railed
  Like foreign sailors, landed in the street
Of seaport town, and with outlandish noise
Of oaths and gibberish frightening girls and boys.

4

Thus came the jocund Spring in Killingworth,
  In fabulous days, some hundred years ago;
And thrifty farmers, as they tilled the earth,
  Heard with alarm the cawing of the crow,
That mingled with the universal mirth,
  Cassandra-like, prognosticating woe;
They shook their heads, and doomed with dreadful words
To swift destruction the whole race of birds.

5

And a town-meeting was convened straightway
  To set a price upon the guilty heads
Of these marauders, who, in lieu of pay,
  Levied blackmail upon the garden beds
And cornfields, and beheld without dismay
  The awful scarecrow, with his fluttering shreds,
The skeleton that waited at their feast,
Whereby their sinful pleasure was increased.

6

Then from his house, a temple painted white,
  With fluted columns, and a roof of red,
The Squire came forth, august and splendid sight!
  Slowly descending, with majestic tread,
Three flights of steps, nor looking left nor right,
  Down the long street he walked, as one who said,
"A town that boasts inhabitants like me
Can have no lack of good society!"

7

The Parson, too, appeared, a man austere,
  The instinct of whose nature was to kill;
The wrath of God he preached from year to year,
  And read, with fervor, Edwards on the Will;
His favorite pastime was to slay the deer
  In Summer on some Adirondack hill;
E'en now, while walking down the rural lane,
He lopped the wayside lilies with his cane.

8

From the Academy, whose belfry crowned
  The Hill of Science with its vane of brass,
Came the Preceptor, gazing idly round,
  Now at the clouds, and now at the green grass,
And all absorbed in reveries profound
  Of fair Almira in the upper class,
Who was, as in a sonnet he had said,
As pure as water and as good as bread.

9

And next the Deacon issued from his door,
  In his voluminous neck-cloth, white as snow;
A suit of sable bombazine he wore;
  His form was ponderous, and his step was slow;
There never was so wise a man before;
  He seemed the incarnate "Well, I told you so!"
And to perpetuate his great renown
There was a street named after him in town.

10

These came together in the new town-hall,
  With sundry farmers from the region round.
The Squire presided, dignified and tall,
  His air impressive and his reasoning sound;
Ill fared it with the birds, both great and small;
  Hardly a friend in all that crowd they found,
But enemies enough, who every one
Charged them with all the crimes beneath the sun.

11

When they had ended, from his place apart,
  Rose the Preceptor, to redress the wrong,
And, trembling like a steed before the start,
  Looked round bewildered on the expectant throng;
Then thought of fair Almira, and took heart
  To speak out what was in him, clear and strong,
Alike regardless of their smile or frown,
And quite determined not to be laughed down.

12

"Plato, anticipating the Reviewers,
　From his Republic banished without pity
The Poets; in this little town of yours,
　You put to death, by means of a Committee,
The ballad-singers and the troubadours,
　The street-musicians of the heavenly city,
The birds, who make sweet music for us all
In our dark hours, as David did for Saul.

13

"The thrush that carols at the dawn of day
　From the green steeples of the piny wood;
The oriole in the elm; the noisy jay,
　Jargoning like a foreigner at his food;
The bluebird balanced on some topmost spray,
　Flooding with melody the neighborhood;
Linnet and meadow-lark, and all the throng
That dwell in nests, and have the gift of song,—

14

"You slay them all! and wherefore? for the gain
　Of a scant handful more or less of wheat,
Or rye, or barley, or some other grain,
　Scratched up at random by industrious feet,
Searching for worm or weevil after rain,
　Or a few cherries, that are not so sweet
As are the songs these uninvited guests
Sing at their feasts with comfortable breasts.

15

"Do you ne'er think what wondrous beings these?
  Do you ne'er think who made them, and who **taught**
The dialect they speak, where melodies
  Alone are the interpreters of thought?
Whose household words are songs in many keys,
  Sweeter than instrument of man e'er caught!
Whose habitations in the tree-tops even
Are half-way houses on the road to heaven!

16

"Think, every morning when the sun peeps through
  The dim, leaf-latticed windows of the grove,
How jubilant the happy birds renew
  Their old, melodious madrigals of love!
And when you think of this, remember, too,
  'T is always morning somewhere, and above
The awakening continents, from shore to shore,
Somewhere the birds are singing evermore.

17

"Think of your woods and orchards without birds!
  Of empty nests that cling to boughs and beams,
As in an idiot's brain remembered words
  Hang empty 'mid the cobwebs of his dreams!
Will bleat of flocks or bellowing of herds
  Make up for the lost music, when your teams
Drag home the stingy harvest, and no more
The feathered gleaners follow to your door?

THE BIRDS OF KILLINGWORTH

18

"What! would you rather see the incessant stir
  Of insects in the windrows of the hay,
And hear the locust and the grasshopper
  Their melancholy hurdy-gurdies play?
Is this more pleasant to you than the whir
  Of meadow-lark, and its sweet roundelay,
Or twitter of little field-fares, as you take
Your nooning in the shade of bush and brake?

19

"You call them thieves and pillagers; but know,
  They are the wingèd wardens of your farms,
Who from the cornfields drive the insidious foe,
  And from your harvests keep a hundred harms;
Even the blackest of them all, the crow,
  Renders good service as your man-at-arms,
Crushing the beetle in his coat of mail,
And crying havoc on the slug and snail.

20

"How can I teach your children gentleness,
  And mercy to the weak, and reverence
For Life, which, in its weakness or excess,
  Is still a gleam of God's omnipotence,
Or Death, which, seeming darkness, is no less
  The selfsame light, although averted hence,
When by your laws, your actions, and your speech,
You contradict the very things I teach?"

21

With this he closed; and through the audience went
    A murmur, like the rustle of dead leaves;
The farmers laughed and nodded, and some bent
    Their yellow heads together like their sheaves;
Men have no faith in fine-spun sentiment
    Who put their trust in bullocks and in beeves.
The birds were doomed; and, as the record shows,
A bounty offered for the heads of crows.

22

There was another audience out of reach,
    Who had no voice nor vote in making laws,
But in the papers read his little speech,
    And crowned his modest temples with applause;
They made him conscious, each one more than each,
    He still was victor, vanquished in their cause.
Sweetest of all, the applause he won from thee,
O fair Almira at the Academy!

23

And so the dreadful massacre began;
    O'er fields and orchards, and o'er woodland crests,
The ceaseless fusillade of terror ran.
    Dead fell the birds, with blood-stains on their breasts,
Or wounded crept away from sight of man,
    While the young died of famine in their nests;
A slaughter to be told in groans, not words,
The very St. Bartholomew of Birds!

24

The Summer came, and all the birds were dead;
　　The days were like hot coals; the very ground
Was burned to ashes; in the orchards fed
　　Myriads of caterpillars, and around
The cultivated fields and garden beds
　　Hosts of devouring insects crawled, and found
No foe to check their march, till they had made
The land a desert without leaf or shade.

25

Devoured by worms, like Herod, was the town,
　　Because, like Herod, it had ruthlessly
Slaughtered the Innocents. From the trees spun down
　　The canker-worms upon the passers-by,
Upon each woman's bonnet, shawl, and gown,
　　Who shook them off with just a little cry;
They were the terror of each favorite walk,
The endless theme of all the village talk.

26

The farmers grew impatient, but a few
　　Confessed their error, and would not complain,
For, after all, the best thing one can do,
　　When it is raining, is to let it rain.
Then they repealed the law, although they knew
　　It would not call the dead to life again;
As school-boys, finding their mistake too late,
Draw a wet sponge across the accusing slate.

27

That year in Killingworth the Autumn came
  Without the light of his majestic look,
The wonder of the falling tongues of flame,
  The illumined pages of his Doomsday book.
A few last leaves blushed crimson with their shame
  And drowned themselves despairing in the brook,
While the wild wind went moaning everywhere,
Lamenting the dead children of the air.

28

But the next Spring a stranger sight was seen,
  A sight that never yet by bard was sung,
As great a wonder as it would have been
  If some dumb animal had found a tongue!
A wagon, overarched with evergreen,
  Upon whose boughs were wicker cages hung,
All full of singing birds, came down the street,
Filling the air with music wild and sweet.

29

From all the country round these birds were brought,
  By order of the town, with anxious quest,
And, loosened from their wicker prisons, sought
  In woods and fields the places they loved best,
Singing loud canticles, which many thought
  Were satires to the authorities addressed,
While others, listening in green lanes, averred
Such lovely music never had been heard.

THE BIRDS OF KILLINGWORTH

30

But blither still and louder carolled they
  Upon the morrow, for they seemed to know
It was fair Almira's wedding-day,
  And everywhere, around, above, below,
When the Preceptor bore his bride away,
  Their songs burst forth in joyous overflow,
And a new heaven bent over a new earth
Amid the sunny farms of Killingworth.

—Henry Wadsworth Longfellow.

Stanza one—*Blithe-heart King*—the joyous Creator.

Stanza two—"Are not two sparrows sold for a farthing? and one of them shall not fall on the ground without your Father. But the very hairs of your head are numbered. Fear ye not therefore; ye are of more value than many sparrows." —*St. Matthew, 10:29-31.*

Stanza two—"Who provideth for the raven his food? When his young ones cry unto God, they wander for lack of meat." —*Job 38:41.* "He giveth to the beast his food *and* to the young ravens which cry."—*Psalms 147:9.*

Cassandra, in Greek mythology, was always prophesying woe, but Apollo had ordered that no credit should ever be attached to her predictions.

At Egyptian feasts, according to Plutarch, a servant brought in a skeleton towards the close and cried aloud to the guests: "Look on this! Eat, drink, and be merry, for tomorrow you die."

The squire, the parson, the schoolmaster, and the deacon were the leading men of any community in early New England days. They are described here quite true to nature. *Edwards on the Will* was Jonathan Edwards' famous book on *Freedom of the Will*. He was a powerful exponent of Calvinistic theology.

Stanza twelve—*Plato*, the greatest of the Athenian philosophers, wrote a scheme of an ideal republic. Various classes were to be excluded, among them the poets. The *Reviewers* refers to the critics in the English and Scotch magazines in the early part of the 19th century whose reviews of new poetry were severe and merciless. The *Troubadours* were a school of lyric poets who flourished in France and Italy, in the 11th, 12th and 13th centuries. Many of them sang or chanted their poems in the streets.

In our dark hours, as David did for Saul—"And it came to pass, when the *evil* spirit from God was upon Saul, that David took an harp, and played with the hand; so Saul was refreshed, and was well, and the evil spirit departed from him."— *First Samuel 16:23*. See also Browning's poem, *Saul*.

Stanza twenty-two—The *other audience* was composed of the women and girls, who were not permitted to attend the town meeting.

Stanza twenty-three—The massacre of St. Bartholomew's Day was the massacre of the Huguenots in France in 1572. The number of victims in Paris was from 3,000 to 10,000, and in all France, between 20,000 and 30,000.

Stanza twenty-five—*Like Herod*—"Then Herod . . . sent forth, and slew all the children that were in Bethlehem, and in all the coasts thereof, from two years old and under."— *St. Matthew, 2:16*.

Stanza twenty-seven—The Doomsday Book was the ancient record of the lands and property in England, made by order of William the Conqueror, about 1086, to determine the taxable property in the country, and the corresponding services due to the crown. Also spelled Domesday (see *page* 168).

The Preceptor's speech for the preservation of the birds is the most important part of the poem, and special attention should be given to it in the study of the piece. Longfellow seems to intimate that the Preceptor's tender feeling for Almira at the Academy had something to do with his attitude towards the birds.

Whenever any kind of bird is mentioned throughout the poem, notice the accurate description of it; for example, "the noisy jay, jargoning like a foreigner at his food." Pick out these descriptions; are you familiar with the birds named? *Merle* and *mavis* are English names for the blackbird and the song-thrush.

THE LIGHT OF OTHER DAYS

No child is able to read *The Light of Other Days* with full understanding. He does not have the experience necessary to interpret it. Only those who have passed far beyond "the smiles, the tears of boyhood's years, the words of love then spoken," and can recall from personal experience "the eyes that shone, now dimmed and gone," will be able to "feel like one who treads alone some banquet hall deserted." May that experience be delayed for all of them for many and many a year! Nevertheless, the poem is a gem of pathetic beauty, and the youth who is familiar with it is sure to find a personal interpretation of it in the future years when memory brings the light of other days around him. It is a good thing to store away in the mind for future use.

THE LIGHT OF OTHER DAYS

1

Oft in the stilly night
  Ere slumber's chain has bound me,
Fond Memory brings the light
  Of other days around me:
    The smiles, the tears
    Of boyhood's years,
  The words of love then spoken;
    The eyes that shone,
    Now dimmed and gone,
  The cheerful hearts now broken!
Thus in the stilly night
  Ere slumber's chain has bound me,
Sad Memory brings the light
  Of other days around me.

2

When I remember all
  The friends so linked together
I've seen around me fall
  Like leaves in wintry weather,
    I feel like one
    Who treads alone
  Some banquet hall deserted,
    Whose lights are fled,
    Whose garlands dead,
  And all but he departed.

Thus in the stilly night
　Ere slumber's chain has bound me,
Sad Memory brings the light
　Of other days around me.

　　　　　　　　　—Thomas Moore.

THE ISLE OF LONG AGO

Children are just starting down the river of Time and as yet they have no isle of Long Ago, that willow-covered spot where most men and women have left so many sacred treasures—things that are now only "heaps of dust, but we love them so!" Children ought not to know from experience that this river of Time "runs through the realm of tears"; and of course they know nothing of "the broken vows and the pieces of rings, and the garments she used to wear." Yet the poem is rich in imagination and melody; and, as in the case of *The Light of Other Days* (page 141), it will be turned to again and again in after years, and they will hear, "through the turbulent roar, sweet voices they heard in the days gone before."

In teaching this poem and *The Light of Other Days* the teacher should explain these things to the children so that they will know that the experience of life will give them, soon enough, the ability to interpret and to understand.

THE ISLE OF LONG AGO

1

Oh, a wonderful stream is the river of Time,
  As it runs through the realm of tears,
With a faultless rhythm and a musical rhyme,
And a boundless sweep and a surge sublime,
  As it blends with the ocean of Years.

2

How the winters are drifting, like flakes of snow,
  And the summers, like buds between;
And the year in the sheaf—so they come and they go,
On the river's breast, with its ebb and flow,
  As it glides in the shadow and sheen.

3

There's a magical isle up the river of Time,
  Where the softest of airs are playing;
There's a cloudless sky and a tropical clime,
And a song as sweet as a vesper chime,
  And the Junes with the roses are staying.

4

And the name of that isle is the Long Ago,
  And we bury our treasures there;

There are brows of beauty and bosoms of snow—
There are heaps of dust—but we love them so!—
　There are trinkets and tresses of hair;

5

There are fragments of song that nobody sings,
　And a part of an infant's prayer,
There's a lute unswept, and a harp without strings;
There are broken vows and pieces of rings,
　And the garments that she used to wear.

6

There are hands that are waved, when the fairy shore
　By the mirage is lifted in air;
And we sometimes hear, through the turbulent roar,
Sweet voices we heard in the days gone before,
　When the wind down the river is fair.

7

Oh, remembered for aye be the blessed Isle,
　All the day of our life till night—
When the evening comes with its beautiful smile,
And our eyes are closing to slumber awhile,
　May that "Greenwood" of Soul be in sight!
　　　　　　　　—Benjamin Franklin Taylor.

Greenwood—a cemetery in Brooklyn, N. Y.
Greenwood of the Soul—means the soul's resting-place, or heaven.

RECESSIONAL

The *Recessional* is a protest and a prayer. It was first published in the London *Times* of July 17, 1897, and the occasion which brought it forth was the diamond jubilee commemorative of Queen Victoria's coronation. The celebration was most magnificent in splendor and extravagant in expense; no Roman conqueror ever witnessed such pageantry. Rejoicing in the worldly pride and power of Britain on sea and land was the chief characteristic of the event, and for the time being any higher power seemed to be forgotten. At the close of the celebration Mr. Rudyard Kipling published the *Recessional,* and it had wonderful effect in sobering the nation and bringing the more thoughtful persons to a true conception of national and personal responsibility. It was read from a multitude of pulpits, and soon everybody was repeating it. No other poem of our time has had such immediate or such deep influence. It is doubtless the greatest hymn of this generation.

The title is fitting. The recessional hymn is the hymn sung after the service as the singers return in procession to the robing room; and Mr. Kipling's poem was written to be read after the celebration.

RECESSIONAL

1

God of our fathers, known of old—
Lord of our far-flung battle-line.

Beneath whose awful hand we hold
   Dominion over palm and pine—
Lord God of Hosts, be with us yet,
Let we forget—lest we forget!

2

The tumult and the shouting dies—
   The captains and the kings depart,
Still stands Thine ancient Sacrifice,
   An humble and a contrite heart—
Lord God of Hosts, be with us yet,
Lest we forget—lest we forget!

3

Far-called, our navies melt away—
   On dune and headland sinks the fire;
Lo! all our pomp of yesterday
   Is one with Nineveh and Tyre!
Judge of the Nations, spare us yet,
Lest we forget—lest we forget!

4

If drunk with sight of power, we loose
   Wild tongues that have not Thee in awe—
Such boasting as the Gentiles use,
   Or lesser breeds, without the law—
Lord God of Hosts, be with us yet,
Lest we forget—lest we forget!

5

For heathen heart that puts its trust
   In reeking tube, and iron shard—
All valiant dust, that builds on dust,
   And guarding calls not Thee to guard—
For frantic boast and foolish word,
Thy mercy on Thy people, Lord!
                  —Rudyard Kipling.

Far-flung battle-line—calls to mind Webster's reference to England's army "whose morning drum-beat, following the sun and keeping company with the hours, encircles the globe with one unbroken strain of the martial airs of England."

Palm and pine—palm typifies the south and pine the north.

The captains and the kings depart—return to their homes after taking part in the jubilee.

Thine ancient Sacrifice, etc.—A familiar Biblical reference.—Psalm 51:17 says, "The sacrifices of God *are* a broken spirit; a broken and a contrite heart, O God, thou wilt not despise."

Far-called, our navies melt away—They had been gathered together for the jubilee and now they depart for their various stations.

On dune and headland sinks the fire—One feature of the celebration was a multitude of bonfires on the hilltops over the country, which could be seen from one to another. Now that the jubilee is ending these fires are permitted to die out.

Lo, all our pomp of yesterday is one with Nineveh and Tyre—gone like them, and it was much like them in spirit, too. Notice the happy use of the word *pomp*.

Loose wild tongues—boasting tongues.

Gentiles and *lesser breeds without the law*—peoples without Christian civilization.

Reeking tube—cannon.

Iron shard—broken pieces of bomb shells.

Valiant dust that builds on dust—courageous men who rely wholly upon their own powers and forget God.

And so we see that the poem is a protest against the spirit of the English nation as shown in the Queen's jubilee, and a prayer to the Judge of Nations for mercy.

THE LADDER OF ST. AUGUSTINE

St. Augustine, Bishop of Hippo, was the most eminent of the Latin Fathers of the Church. He was born November 13, 354, in Numidia (the eastern half of modern Algeria), and died 430. He lived at Carthage, Rome, Milan, and Hippo. During his youth and early manhood he was guilty of many excesses, vices, and follies. Years later, in one of his sermons he used the expression, *"De vitiis nostris scalam nobis facimus, si vitia ipsa calcamus"* (of our vices we make for ourselves a ladder, if we trample them under foot). None knew better than St. Augustine the truth of this from his own experiences. Longfellow takes the thought and elaborates it into a familiar poem. He gives a catalogue of vices, each one of which may be made to serve as a round in the ladder; but to become such it must be put under foot. Pupils should make a list of these "rounds of the ladder" and discuss them in class.

Any good picture of the Egyptian pyramids will show how true the description is in stanza eight.

THE LADDER OF ST. AUGUSTINE

1

Saint Augustine! well hast thou said,
  That of our vices we can frame
A ladder, if we will but tread
  Beneath our feet each deed of shame!

2

All common things, each day's events
  That with the hour begin and end;
Our pleasures and our discontents,
  Are rounds by which we may ascend.

3

The low desire, the base design,
  That makes another's virtues less;
The revel of the giddy wine,
  And all occasions of excess;

4

The longing for ignoble things,
  The strife for triumph more than truth,
The hardening of the heart, that brings
  Irreverence for the dreams of youth;

THE LADDER OF ST. AUGUSTINE

5

All thoughts of ill—all evil deeds
  That have their root in thoughts of ill;
Whatever hinders or impedes
  The action of the nobler will;—

6

All these must first be trampled down
  Beneath our feet, if we would gain
In the bright field of fair renown
  The right of eminent domain!

7

We have not wings, we cannot soar,
  But we have feet to scale and climb
By slow degrees—by more and more—
  The cloudy summits of our time.

8

The mighty pyramids of stone
  That wedge-like cleave the desert airs,
When nearer seen and better known,
  Are but gigantic flights of stairs.

9

The distant mountains that uprear
  Their frowning foreheads to the skies,
Are crossed by pathways that appear
  As we to higher levels rise.

10

The heights by great men reached and kept,
    Were not attained by sudden flight;
But they, while their companions slept,
    Were toiling upward in the night.

11

Standing on what too long we bore
    With shoulders bent and downcast eyes,
We may discern, unseen before,
    A path to higher destinies.

12

Nor deem the irrevocable past
    As wholly wasted, wholly vain,
If, rising on its wrecks, at last
    To something nobler we attain.

—Henry Wadsworth Longfellow.

The right of eminent domain (stanza six)—the right of supreme control for the good of ourselves and others. Technically it means the right of a government or a state over all the property within the state to appropriate any part thereof to a necessary public use, reasonable compensation being made.

The thought which Longfellow uses in this poem is similar to that used by Tennyson in the first stanza of *In Memoriam*:

> I held it truth, with him who sings
>   To one clear harp in divers tones,
>   That men may rise on stepping-stones
> Of their dead selves to higher things.

And J. G. Holland has two verses in a similar vein in his poem *Gradatim:*

> Heaven is not reached at a single bound;
> But we build the ladder by which we rise
> From the lowly earth to the vaulted skies,
> And we mount to the summit round by round.
>
> We rise by things that are under our feet;
> By what we have mastered of good and gain;
> By the pride deposed and the passion slain,
> And the vanquished ills that we hourly meet.

ICHABOD

The Biblical name Ichabod ("Ichabod, the glory is departed") is here applied by Whittier to Daniel Webster. Whittier was the foremost of the anti-slavery poets, and Webster was regarded as the great defender of the Union against the doctrine of states' rights. But when Webster made his speech in 1850 in defense of a fugitive slave law, his friends at the North regarded it as a bid for southern support in his candidacy for the presidential nomination, and as little short of treason to the Union cause. Immediately after the speech of Webster's, Whittier wrote the poem *Ichabod,* expressing his own feelings and the feelings of the North towards Webster's changed attitude. Thirty years later Whittier wrote *The Lost Occasion,* in which he made amends for whatever injustice *Ichabod* might have done to the character of the great orator and statesman.

Ichabod is one of the strongest of Whittier's poems, and the finest lines in it are, perhaps,

> . . . his dim, dishonored brow,

and the last two lines of the eighth stanza,

> When faith is lost, when honor dies,
> The man is dead!

The last two lines of the poem have reference to the incident narrated in *Genesis 9, verses 20-23:*

> And Noah began *to be* a husbandman, and he planted a vineyard:
> And he drank of the wine, and was drunken; and he was uncovered within his tent.
> And Ham, the father of Canaan, saw the nakedness of his father, and told his two brethren without.
> And Shem and Japheth took a garment, and laid *it* upon both their shoulders, and went backward, and covered the nakedness of their father; and their faces *were* backward, and they saw not their father's nakedness.

Read Whittier's *The Lost Occasion.*

ICHABOD

1

So fallen! so lost! the light withdrawn
    Which once he wore!
The glory from his gray hairs gone
    Forevermore!

2

Revile him not, the Tempter hath
    A snare for all;
And pitying tears, not scorn and wrath,
    Befit his fall!

ICHABOD

3

O, dumb be passion's stormy rage,
    When he who might
Have lighted up and led his age
    Falls back in night!

4

Scorn! would the angels laugh, to mark
    A bright soul driven,
Fiend-goaded, down the endless dark,
    From hope and heaven!

5

Let not the land once proud of him
    Insult him now,
Nor brand with deeper shame his dim,
    Dishonored brow.

6

But let its humble sons, instead,
    From sea to lake,
A long lament, as for the dead,
    In sadness make.

7

Of all we loved and honored, naught
    Save power remains;
A fallen angel's pride of thought,
    Still strong in chains.

8

All else is gone; from those great eyes
    The soul has fled;
When faith is lost, when honor dies,
    The man is dead!

9

Then pay the reverence of old days
    To his dead fame;
Walk backward, with averted gaze,
    And hide the shame!

—John Greenleaf Whittier.

THE BUGLE SONG
From *The Princess.*

The poem was inspired by the echoes on the lake at Killarney, during Tennyson's visit there in 1847.

All persons who have lived among the hills or the mountains have had delightful experiences with echoes, and a discussion of these experiences would be a good introduction to the study of this poem. Wonderful stories are told of the number of times an echo has repeated itself. Of the memories of childhood these are often among the most treasured.

> Somewhere among these stoic rocks,
>   Or hidden in this cloistered dell,
> Shut in by Time's unyielding locks,
>   Lost echoes of my boyhood dwell.

But the mountain echo is unlike our personal echoes or influence. The physical echo becomes fainter and fainter, and finally ceases entirely, but our influence goes on forever. And so the meaning, the significance, of the poem is expressed in the lines in the third stanza:

> Our echoes roll from soul to soul,
> And grow forever and forever.

Substitute the word *influence* for the word *echoes* in the first of these two lines, and the meaning of the poem is revealed. But too much emphasis should not be placed upon the "moral" of this beautiful little lyric. The pleasure given by the first two stanzas is worth as much, perhaps, as the lesson in the third.

THE BUGLE SONG

1

The splendor falls on castle walls
  And snowy summits old in story;
The long light shakes across the lakes,
  And the wild cataract leaps in glory.
Blow, bugle, blow! set the wild echoes flying.
Blow, bugle! answer, echoes! dying, dying, **dying.**

2

O hark! O hear, how thin and clear,
  And thinner, clearer, farther going!
O sweet and far, from cliff and scar,
  The horns of Elf-land faintly blowing!

Blow! let us hear the purple glens replying.
Blow, bugle! answer, echoes! dying, dying, dying.

3

O love, they die in yon rich sky,
    They faint on hill, or field, or river.
Our echoes roll from soul to soul,
    And grow forever and forever.
Blow, bugle, blow! set the wild echoes flying.
And answer, echoes, answer! dying, dying, dying.
                      —Alfred Tennyson.

Scar — a steep, rocky eminence.

WHERE LIES THE LAND?

The voyage of life is a favorite theme in poetry, and it is vividly pictured here. Life is pleasant when one has friends and the sun shines and the way is smooth (stanza two). The brave-hearted even get pleasure out of life's storms and struggles (stanza three). But whence we came and where we go are alike unknown. It is a poem of doubt, but not of despair.

WHERE LIES THE LAND?

1

Where lies the land to which the ship would go?
Far, far ahead, is all her seamen know.
And where the land she travels from? Away,
Far, far behind, is all that they can say.

2

On sunny noons upon the deck's smooth face,
Linked arm in arm, how pleasant here to pace;
Or, o'er the stern reclining, watch below
The foaming wake far widening as we go.

3

On stormy nights, when wild northwesters rave,
How proud a thing to fight with wind and wave!
The dripping sailor on the reeling mast
Exults to bear, and scorns to wish it past.

4

Where lies the land to which the ship would go?
Far, far ahead, is all her seamen know.
And where the land she travels from? Away,
Far, far behind, is all that they can say.
—Arthur Hugh Clough.

THE RHODORA

The thought in this beautiful and perfect little poem is similar to the thought in Tennyson's *Flower in the Crannied Wall:*

> Flower in the crannied wall,
>   I pluck you out of the crannies,
> I hold you here, root and all, in my hand,
> Little flower,—but *if* I could understand
> What you are, root and all, and all in all,
>   I should know what God and man is.

They present the idea of the unity of all things. Emerson makes Nature say, in *The Sphinx,* "Who telleth one of my meanings is master of all I am." This is the central theme of *The Rhodora.*

Longfellow, speaking of Emerson, says:

> It was his faith, perhaps is mine,
> That life in all its forms is one.

A secondary thought is stated in the line, "Beauty is its own excuse for being." This is a thoroughly sound and thoroughly useful principle, but one which the world has not fully accepted, at least in practice.

THE RHODORA

In May, when sea-winds pierced our solitudes,
I found the fresh Rhodora in the woods,
Spreading its leafless blooms in a damp nook,
To please the desert and the sluggish brook.
The purple petals, fallen in the pool,
Made the black water with their beauty gay;
Here might the redbird come his plumes to cool,
And court the flower that cheapens his array.
Rhodora! if the sages ask thee why
This charm is wasted on the earth and sky,
Tell them, dear, that if eyes were made for seeing,
Then beauty is its own excuse for being.

Why thou wert there, O rival of the rose!
I never thought to ask, I never knew:
But, in my simple ignorance, suppose
  The selfsame Power that brought me there brought you. —Ralph Waldo Emerson.

The *Rhodora* belongs to the Rhododendron family and is a native of cold and wet wooded places from Pennsylvania north. It has delicate rosy flowers which appear before the leaves.

THE FINDING OF THE LYRE

This is an allegory and tells in simple rhyme an old and familiar truth—the world is full of music and beauty and opportunity, all about us every day. But most of us fail to see or hear or understand. The man of genius, whether poet, musician, inventor, or philosopher, is the one who discovers them, interprets them, and puts them to use.

THE FINDING OF THE LYRE

1

There lay upon the ocean's shore
  What once a tortoise served to cover;
A year and more, with rush and roar,
  The surf had rolled it over,
Had played with it, and flung it by,
  As wind and weather might decide it,
Then tossed it high where sand-drifts dry
  Cheap burial might provide it.

2

It rested there, to bleach or tan;
   The rains had soaked, the suns had burned it;
With many a ban the fisherman
   Had stumbled o'er and spurned it;
And there the fisher girl would stay,
   Conjecturing with her brother
How in their play the poor estray
   Might serve some use or other.

3

So there it lay, through wet and dry,
   As empty as the last new sonnet,
Till by and by came Mercury,
   And having mused upon it,
"Why, here," cried he, "the thing of things
   In shape, material, and dimensions!
Give it but strings, and, lo, it sings,
   A wonderful invention!"

4

So said, so done; the chords he strained,
   And as his fingers o'er them hovered,
The shell disdained, a soul had gained,
   The lyre had been discovered.
O empty world that round us lies,
   Dead shell, of soul and thought forsaken,
Brought we but eyes like Mercury's,
   In thee what songs should waken!

                        —James Russell Lowell.

Mercury—in classic mythology, was the supposed inventor of the lyre, and of weights and measures. He was also the messenger of the gods.

As empty as the last new sonnet—referring to the poor quality of current poetry.

THE SANDS O' DEE

The meaning of genuine poetry can never be fully expressed in prose. Poetry appeals to the emotions, and part of the appeal is made through the rhythm, the "music," of the lines. The haunting melody of Poe's *Annabel Lee,* for example, creates an emotion of pleasure quite apart from the meaning of the verses.

The three qualities of Charles Kingsley's little poem *The Sands o' Dee* are imagination, melody, and mystery. A young girl goes to call the cattle home from the marshes of the River Dee where it flows into the Irish Sea; in the blinding mist and the wet western wind she loses her way, the tide comes creeping up and carries her out among the fishermen's nets. By her golden hair she is recognized, for no salmon ever shone so fair. The tragedy so appeals to the fishermen that their natural superstition leads them to imagine that they still sometimes hear her voice across the sands o' Dee going as of old to call the cattle home. Thus a legend, such as is the basis of the story in the poem, arises.

These things are treated with so much imagination and melody, and the mysterious element is so closely and artistically woven in with the rest of the poem, that the total effect is wholly different from that which any mere prose statement could create. Imagination, melody, mystery—by the use of these three elements Kingsley has taken a familiar tragedy of the sea and converted it into a haunting poem which one can never forget. But in reading a poem like this one either feels its meaning or he doesn't; and no interpreter can be of any great assistance to him.

THE SANDS O' DEE

1

"O Mary, go and call the cattle home,
    And call the cattle home,
    And call the cattle home,
  Across the sands o' Dee."
The western wind was wild and dark wi' foam,
  And all alone went she.

2

The western tide crept up along the sand,
    And o'er and o'er the sand,
    And round and round the sand,
  As far as eye could see;
The rolling mist came down and hid the land;
  And never home came she.

3

"O, is it weed, or fish, or floating hair—
    A tress o' golden hair,
    O' drowned maiden's hair,
  Above the nets at sea?"
Was never salmon yet that shone so fair
  Among the stakes on Dee.

4

They rowed her in across the rolling foam,
    The cruel, crawling foam,
    The cruel, hungry foam,
  To her grave beside the sea.
But still the boatmen hear her call the cattle home,
  Across the sands o' Dee.

          —Charles Kingsley.

ABOU BEN ADHEM

This poem, in imitation of an oriental fable, may be or it may not be good theology, but it expresses the modern idea of altruism which is the basis of all social service. "For he that loveth not his brother whom he hath seen, how can he love God whom he hath not seen?" It has taken the world a long time to learn that "the second commandment is like unto the first." Perhaps Leigh Hunt's simple poem, known and quoted everywhere, has helped a little to turn the minds of men toward the needs of their fellowmen. Doubtless these eighteen lines have built more than one hospital and sent more than one angel of mercy to the children of the slums. "And the King shall answer and say unto them, Verily I say unto you, inasmuch as ye have done it unto one of the least of these, my brethren, ye have done it unto me."

ABOU BEN ADHEM

1

Abou Ben Adhem (may his tribe increase!)
Awoke one night from a deep dream of peace,
And saw within the moonlight in his room,
Making it rich and like a lily in bloom,
An angel writing in a book of gold.

2

Exceeding peace had made Ben Adhem bold;
And to the presence in the room he said,
"What writest thou?" The vision raised its head,
And, with a look made of all sweet accord,
Answered, "The names of those who love the Lord."

3

"And is mine one?" said Abou. "Nay, not so,"
Replied the angel. Abou spoke more low,
But cheerly still; and said, "I pray thee, then,
Write me as one that loves his fellow-men."

The angel wrote, and vanished. The next night
It came again, with a great wakening light,
And showed the names whom love of God had blessed;
And, lo! Ben Adhem's name led all the rest.
                              —Leigh Hunt.

GILLESPIE

Vellore is a town in British India situated in the district of North Arcot on the right bank of the River Palár.

After the fall of Seringapatam (1799) Vellore became the residence of the sons of Tippoo Sahib, the dethroned Sultan of Mysore. Owing to the intrigues of these sons of Tippoo Sahib, a revolt of the sepoys was begun on the 10th of July, 1806.

The insurgents were quickly subdued by Colonel Gillespie, the gallant commander of the British forces stationed at Vellore, which was the military cantonment of the North Arcot district of the Madras presidency. About eight hundred sepoys were put to the sword.

Mr. Newbolt's poem is not only dramatic but it is thoroughly and unusually alive with so-called local coloring. It is one of the best things of its kind in any tongue.

GILLESPIE

1

Riding at dawn, riding alone,
    Gillespie left the town behind;
Before he turned by the westward road
    A horseman crossed him, staggering blind.

2

"The devil's abroad in false Vellore—
    The devil that stabs by night," he said:
"Women and children, rank and file,
    Dying and dead, dying and dead."

3

Without a word, without a groan,
    Sudden and swift Gillespie turned;
The blood roared in his ears like fire,
    Like fire the road beneath him burned.

4

He thundered back to Arcot gate,
    He thundered up through Arcot town;
Before he thought a second thought
    In the barrack yard he lighted down.

5

"Trumpeter, sound for the Light Dragoons!
    Sound to saddle and spur!" he said.
"He that is ready may ride with me,
And he that can may ride ahead."

GILLESPIE.

6

Fierce and fain, fierce and fain,
  Behind him went the troopers grim;
They rode as ride the Light Dragoons,
  But never a man could ride with him.

7

Their rowels ripped their horses' sides,
  Their hearts were red with a deeper goad,
But ever alone before them all
  Gillespie rode, Gillespie rode.

8

Alone he came to false Vellore;
  The walls were lined, the gates were barred;
Alone he walked where the bullets bit,
  And called above to the sergeant's guard:

9

"Sergeant, sergeant, over the gate,
  Where are your officers, all?" he said.
Heavily came the sergeant's voice,
  "There are two living and forty dead."

10

"A rope, a rope!" Gillespie cried,
  They bound their belts to serve his need.
There was not a rebel behind the wall
  But laid his barrel and drew his bead.

11

There was not a rebel among them all
  But pulled his trigger and cursed his aim,

For lightly swung and rightly swung,
  Over the gate Gillespie came.

12

He dressed the line, he led the charge;
  They swept the wall like a stream in spate,
And roaring over the roar they heard
  The galloper guns that burst the gate.

13

Fierce and fain, fierce and fain,
  The troopers rode the reeking flight;
The very stones remember still
  The end of them that stab by night.

14

They've kept the tale a hundred years,
  They'll keep the tale a hundred more;
Riding at dawn, riding alone,
  Gillespie came to false Vellore.

—Henry Newbolt.

EXCELSIOR

Longfellow, in a letter to Mr. Tuckerman, wrote the following interpretation of the poem:

"I have had the pleasure of receiving your note in regard to the poem 'Excelsior,' and very willingly give you my intention in writing it. This was no more than to display, in a series of pictures, the life of a man of genius, resisting all temptations, laying aside all fears, heedless of all warnings and pressing right on to accomplish his purpose. His motto is *Excelsior,* 'higher.' He passes through the Alpine village—through the rough, cold paths of the world—where the peasants cannot understand him, and where his watchword is an 'unknown tongue.' He disregards the happiness of domestic peace, and sees the glaciers—his fate—before him. He disregards the warnings of the old man's wisdom and the fascinations of woman's love. He answers to all, 'higher yet.' The monks of Saint Bernard are the representatives of religious forms and ceremonies, and with their oft-repeated prayer mingles the sound of his voice, telling them there is something higher than forms and ceremonies. Filled with these aspirations he perishes, without having reached the perfection he longed for; and the voice in the air is the promise of immortality and progress ever upward."

EXCELSIOR

1

The shades of night were falling fast,
As through an Alpine village passed
A youth, who bore 'mid snow and ice,
A banner with the strange device,
    "Excelsior!"

2

His brow was sad; his eye beneath
Flashed like a falchion from its sheath;
And like a silver clarion rung
The accents of that unknown tongue,
        "Excelsior!"

3

In happy homes he saw the light
Of household fires gleam warm and bright;
Above, the spectral glaciers shone,
And from his lips escaped a groan,
        "Excelsior!"

4

"Try not to pass," the old man said;
"Dark lowers the tempest overhead,
The roaring torrent is deep and wide!"
And loud that clarion voice replied,
        "Excelsior!"

5

"O stay," the maiden said, "and rest
Thy weary head upon this breast!"
A tear stood in his bright blue eye,
But still he answered with a sigh,
        "Excelsior!"

6

"Beware the pine tree's withered branch!
Beware the awful avalanche!"
This was the peasant's last good-night.
A voice replied, far up the height,
"Excelsior!"

7

At break of day, as heavenward
The pious monks of Saint Bernard
Uttered the oft-repeated prayer,
A voice cried through the startled air,
"Excelsior!"

8

A traveler, by the faithful hounds,
Half-buried in the snow, was found,
Still grasping in his hand of ice
That banner with the strange device,
"Excelsior!"

9

There in the twilight cold and gray,
Lifeless but beautiful he lay,
And from the sky serene and far
A voice fell, like a falling star,
"Excelsior!"

—Henry Wadsworth Longfellow.

THE ISLES OF GREECE
Don Juan, Canto III

This lyric is found in Don Juan, a long poem which shows Byron at his best and his worst. It shows his versatile genius at its height.

The setting of the song in the long poem is as follows: Don Juan, the hero of the story, in his wanderings, has been wrecked off the coast of Greece and cast unconscious upon the beach. He is found by Haidee, a beautiful Greek girl, the daughter of a wealthy sea pirate, Lombro, and is concealed by her in a cave near the shore. She comes to him day by day, and, with the assistance of her maid, nurses him back to health. Her father goes away to "fleece the flags of many nations." He meets storms and other disasters, and is detained many months. Haidee thinks that her father has been drowned or killed, and, not fearing his return, invites Don Juan to Lombro's mansion, where they live in splendor. As a climax to their joyous life they plan an elaborate banquet and are in the midst of its merriment when the father returns. What follows the coming of Lombro is another story.

Besides the diversions at the banquet offered by dwarfs and dancing girls, a poet of great fame is called upon to sing. The song that he sings is *The Isles of Greece.*

He sings of "the glory that was Greece," and contrasts her former honor with her modern degeneracy. Although the spirits of those who drove out the Persian invaders are ready to rise and fight for the independence of their country, the living, in cowardice, are dumb.

Byron makes the poet sing a song that came from his own heart. At the time these lines were written Greece was struggling to free herself from Turkish tyranny. Byron's consecration to the cause of Greek independence proves how sincerely he felt the emotions presented in these stanzas. Three years after this time he gave his life for the Greek cause. Through the good services of England, France, and Russia, five years after his death Greece was made free.

The poem is valuable for its strong patriotic emotion, its suggestive and illuminating classical references, its appeal to the imagination, its pleasing rhythm, its graceful phrasing, and for the beauty of its general conception.

The poet begins to sing his song under the inspiration of the golden days of Greece, but must change his theme to a complaint that modern Greece is too degenerate to fight for her liberties. He feels yet enough of the old patriotism to blush for such a dishonored country. But there is no hope, and he wishes that he may be placed on "Sunium's marble steep," where he may sing his "swan-song" to the waves—and the world, and die—of grief for the lost liberty of Greece—of shame for his degenerate people.

THE ISLES OF GREECE

1

The isles of Greece, the isles of Greece!
　Where burning Sapho lived and sung,
Where grew the arts of war and peace,
　Where Delos rose, and Phœbus sprung!
Eternal summer gilds them yet,
But all except their sun is set.

2

The Scian and the Teian muse,
　The hero's harp, the lover's lute,
Have found the fame your shores refuse;
　Their place of birth alone is mute
To sounds that echo further west
Than your sires' "Islands of the Blest."

3

The mountains look on Marathon—
　And Marathon looks on the sea;
And musing there an hour alone,
　I dream'd that Greece might still be **free**;
For standing on the Persian's grave,
I could not deem myself a slave.

4

A king sate on the rocky brow
　Which looks o'er sea-borne Salamis;

And ships, by thousands, lay below,
  And men in nations;—all were his!
He counted them at break of day—
And when the sun set, where were they?

5

And where are they? And where art thou,
  My country? On thy voiceless shore
The heroic lay is tuneless now—
  The heroic bosom beats no more!
And must thy lyre, so long divine,
Degenerate into hands like mine?

6

'T is something, in the dearth of fame,
  Though linked among a fetter'd race,
To feel at least a patriot's shame,
  Even, as I sing, suffuse my face;
For what is left the poet here?
For Greece to blush—for Greece a tear.

7

Must *we* but weep o'er days more blest?
  Must *we* but blush? Our fathers bled.
Earth! render back from out thy breast
  A remnant of our Spartan dead!
Of the three hundred grant but three,
To make a new Thermopylæ!

8

What, silent still? and silent all?
   Ah, no;—the voices of the dead
Sound like a distant torrent's fall,
   And answer, "Let one living head,
But one arise—we come, we come!"
'T is but the living who are dumb.

*   *   *   *   *

9

You have the Pyrrhic dance as yet—
   Where is the Pyrrhic phalanx gone?
Of two such lessons, why forget
   The nobler and the manlier one?
You have the letters Cadmus gave—
Think ye he meant them for a slave?

*   *   *   *   *

10

Place me on Sunium's marble steep,
   Where nothing save the waves and I
May hear our mutual murmurs sweep;
   There, swan-like, let me sing and die:
A land of slaves shall ne'er be mine—
Dash down yon cup of Samian wine!

                        —George Gordon Byron.

THE ISLES OF GREECE

Sapho—the lyric poetess of Lesbos, who lived in the seventh century B. C. Only fragments of her poetry have come down to us, but they are fervid enough to justify the epithet "burning."

Delos—an island in the Ægean sea, which was supposed to have risen from the sea. It was the birth-place of Phœbus Apollo.

Scian and *Teian*—refer to Homer and Anacreon. Scio is one of the towns which claim to be Homer's birthplace, and Teos is the birthplace of the lyric poet, Anacreon.

Islands of the Blest—The classic tradition about these islands was doubtless based upon the tale of some adventurous voyager who sailed as far west as the Cape Verde Islands, or the Canaries.

Marathon—a village on the east coast of Attica, memorable as the scene of the defeat of the Persians under Darius by the Greeks under Miltiades, 490 B. C.

Salamis—a small island of Greece off the coast of Attica, noted chiefly for the great naval battle fought there.

A king sate, etc.—This refers to King Xerxes and the battle of Salamis, a great naval battle between the Greeks and Persians, 480 B. C. The Persians were utterly overthrown. Byron doubtless got a suggestion for this stanza from lines from Æschylus, the Greek poet:

> Deep were the groans of Xerxes, when he saw
> This havoc; for his seat, a lofty mound
> Commanding the wide sea, o'erlooked the hosts.
> With rueful cries he rent his royal robes,
> And through his troops embattled on the shore
> Gave signal of retreat; then started wild
> And fled disordered.

Must we but weep, etc.—The feeling expressed in this stanza is sincere, for shortly after the time this poem was written Byron consecrated himself to the cause of Greek independence

Thermopylæ—a famous pass leading from Thessaly into Locris, and the only road by which an invading army can go from northern to southern Greece. It was the scene of the heroic death of Leonidas and his 300 Spartans in their attempt to stem the tide of Persian invasion, 480 B. C.

Pyrrhic dance—the movements of this dance are in imitation of the motions of a combatant. It is said to be named from its inventor, Pyrrhicus.

Pyrrhic phalanx—a formation of troops in battle named after Pyrrhus, king of Epirus.

Cadmus—is fabled to have brought the alphabet from Egypt to Greece.

Sunium—the ancient name of Cape Colonna, the southernmost point of Attica, Greece. Its summit is crowned by the ruins of a temple, 269 feet above the level of the sea, of which 16 columns of white marble are still standing.

Swan-like—the swan is fabled to sing as it is dying; a "swan-song" is a death song.

ON FIRST LOOKING INTO CHAPMAN'S HOMER

The wonderful English boy-poet Keats was not a Greek scholar, though he possessed much of the Greek spirit. One night a friend brought to him a copy of Homer's *Odyssey* translated by George Chapman, and they sat up together all night reading it. They parted at daybreak and his friend went to his lodgings two miles away. At ten o'clock that morning his friend found the sonnet, *On First Looking into Chapman's*

Homer, lying on his library table. Keats had evidently written it before going to sleep after the night's reading.

ON FIRST LOOKING INTO CHAPMAN'S HOMER

Much have I travell'd in the realms of gold,
    And many goodly states and kingdoms seen;
    Round many western islands have I been,
Which bards in fealty to Apollo hold.
Oft of one wide expanse had I been told
    That deep-brow'd Homer ruled as his demesne;
    Yet did I never breathe its pure serene
Till I heard Chapman speak out loud and bold:
    Then felt I like some watcher of the skies
When a new planet swims into his ken;
    Or like stout Cortez when with eagle eyes
He star'd at the Pacific—and all his men
    Look'd at each other with a wild surmise—
Silent, upon a peak in Darien.

—John Keats.

He had travelled in the poetic "realms of gold" only in his imagination and his reading, and had seen "goodly states and kingdoms" only in the same way, for he had never been out of England. His reading had been confined largely to the poets of England, the "western islands." Apollo was the mythical god of music and poetry, and thus the ruler of these "realms of gold" which the poets held in fealty, loyalty, to him as vassals did in the old feudal days. The pictures of Homer all show him as "deep-browed."

Serene—is here used as a noun, meaning calm and clear atmosphere. Every schoolboy knows that it was Balboa and not Cortez who discovered the Pacific Ocean, but this slip does not really mar the beauty and majesty of the figure.

Leigh Hunt says of the last line: "We leave the reader standing upon it, with all the illimitable world of thought and feeling before him, to which his imagination will have brought him, while journeying through these 'realms of gold.'"

Whether the reader has such thoughts and feelings is a good test of whether or not he has read with the understanding.

Keats was only twenty-one when he wrote the sonnet.

BREAK, BREAK, BREAK

Some readers will find in this lyric of Tennyson's a mood of sorrow, others a cry of grief; which, will depend upon how fully the reader can experience for himself the emotion of the author. To those who can enter completely into the spirit of the piece, the breaking of the waves of the sea is like the breaking of the heart.

BREAK, BREAK, BREAK

1

Break, break, break,
  On thy cold gray stones, O sea!
And I would that my tongue could utter
  The thoughts that arise in me.

2

O well for the fisherman's boy,
　　That he shouts with his sister at play!
O well for the sailor lad,
　　That he sings in his boat on the bay!

3

And the stately ships go on
　　To their haven under the hill;
But O for the touch of a vanish'd hand,
　　And the sound of a voice that is still!

4

Break, break, break,
　　At the foot of thy crags, O sea!
But the tender grace of a day that is dead
　　Will never come back to me.

　　　　　　　　　　—Alfred Tennyson.

In the *first stanza* the author says that the breaking waves give him thoughts which he cannot utter. This is the most evident meaning of the poem, that emotion is too deep for any words to express. That the thoughts are sad ones is evident from the three words, "cold gray stones." The sight of breaking waves is often a joyous sight, but not so here.

Stanzas two and *three* tell why. The fisherman's boy is too young to know, and the cheerful sailor lad does not think of the tragedies of those who "go down to the sea in ships." It is well for them that they sing and shout now, for their own fathers may perchance be the next to lose their lives. The stately ships go on to their haven under the hill, but in some

home on the shore there is a woman waiting for the touch of
a vanished hand and the sound of a voice that is still.

In these first three stanzas the tragedy of the sea—the story
of its awful sacrifice of life—is told with marvelous effect.

The thought in the *fourth stanza* grows out of the thought
in the other three. "The tender grace of a day that is dead,"
means some love or joy or happiness of a former time which
can never return. As the sailor comes not back from the sea,
so the lost joy comes not back from the past. And as the sea
breaks on its cold gray stones, so the heart breaks on the crags
of grief. Thus the closing stanza widens the scope of the
meaning of the poem to include all those who lament the tender grace of a day that is dead; and its pathos appeals to all
mankind.

The death of Tennyson's friend, Arthur Hallam, inspired
this poem as well as *In Memoriam* and other tributes.

TUBAL CAIN

Tubal Cain is the Biblical and legendary father of
"all such as forge copper and iron." He was of the
seventh generation in descent from Cain. *Genesis,
Chapter 4, verse 22,* says:

> "And Zillah, she also bare Tubal-Cain, an instructor of
> every artificer in brass and iron."

Ezekiel, Chapter 27, verse 13, uses the name Tubal
in connection with the trading of vessels of brass.

Josephus, in *The Antiquities of the Jews,* says:

> "But Tubal exceeded all men in strength, and was very
> expert and famous in martial performances * * *
> and first of all invented the art of working brass."

TUBAL CAIN

Charles Mackay's poem is an epitome of the history of civilization. In the ages of savagery and barbarism the man who could best wield the spear and the sword was actually king and lord, or chief. As civilization progressed the arts of peace were recognized and war became less honorable. Agriculture was the first of the arts of peace to receive attention, and so the plowshare was invented. To-day civilization has so far advanced that war is no longer honorable except when a people's rights are invaded or "oppression lifts its head."

Tubal Cain in this poem typifies humanity in its progress towards civilization.

TUBAL CAIN

1

Old Tubal Cain was a man of might,
   In days when earth was young;
By the fierce red light of his furnace bright,
   The strokes of his hammer rung:
And he lifted high his brawny hand
   On the iron glowing clear,
Till the sparks rushed out in scarlet showers,
   As he fashioned the sword and the spear.
And he sang: "Hurrah for my handiwork!
   Hurrah for the spear and the sword!
Hurrah for the hand that shall wield them well,
   For he shall be king and lord!"

2

To Tubal Cain came many a one,
  As he wrought by his roaring fire,
And each one prayed for a strong steel blade
  As the crown of his desire,
And he made them weapons sharp and strong,
  Till they shouted loud for glee,
And gave him gifts of pearls and gold,
  And spoils of the forest free.
And they sang: "Hurrah for Tubal Cain,
  Who hath given us strength anew!
Hurrah for the smith, hurrah for the fire,
  And hurrah for the metal true!"

3

But a sudden change came o'er his heart,
  Ere the setting of the sun,
And Tubal Cain was filled with pain
  For the evil he had done;
He saw that men, with rage and hate,
  Made war upon their kind;
That the land was red with the blood they shed,
  In their lust for carnage blind;
And he said, "Alas! that ever I made,
  Or that skill of mine should plan,
The spear and the sword for men whose joy
  Is to slay their fellowman!"

4

And for many a day old Tubal Cain
  Sat brooding o'er his woe;
And his hand forbore to smite the ore,
  And his furnace smoldered low.
But he rose at last with a cheerful face,
  And a bright, courageous eye,
And bared his strong right arm for work,
  While the quick flames mounted high.
And he sang, "Hurrah for my handiwork!"
  As the red sparks lit the air;
"Not alone for the blade was the bright steel made,"—
  And he fashioned the first plowshare.

5

And men, taught wisdom from the past,
  In friendship joined their hands,
Hung the sword in the hall, the spear on the wall,
  And plowed the willing lands;
And sang, "Hurrah for Tubal Cain!
  Our staunch good friend is he;
And for the plowshare and the plow,
  To him our praise shall be.
But while oppression lifts its head,
  Or a tyrant would be lord,
Though we may thank him for the plow,
  We'll not forget the sword."

—Charles Mackay.

THE RAVEN

There have been all sorts of curious and fantastic interpretations of *The Raven*. It has been called a poem of remorse, the ebony bird being the personification of Poe's regret for a misspent life; it has been called a prophecy of evil for the future, springing out of reflections upon his way of living; and various other curious meanings have been read into the verses.

There does not seem to be any reason for going so far to seek its interpretation. Poe himself, in his *Philosophy of Composition*, gives the meaning and method of *The Raven*. He says:

"The death of a beautiful woman is, unquestionably, the most poetical topic in the world—and equally it is beyond doubt that the lips best suited for such topic are those of a bereaved lover. . . . I had now to combine the two ideas of a lover lamenting his deceased mistress and a raven continuously repeating the word 'Nevermore' "—the raven, as he says, being generally considered a bird of ill omen, and the word involving "the utmost conceivable amount of sorrow and despair."

"I determined then to place the lover in his chamber —in a chamber rendered sacred to him by memories of her who had frequented it.

"I made the night tempestuous, first to account for a raven's seeking admission, and secondly, for the effect of contrast with the (physical) serenity within the chamber. I made the bird alight on the bust of Pallas, also for the effect of contrast between the marble and the plumage—the bust of Pallas being chosen, first, as most in keeping with the scholarship of the lover, and, secondly, for the sonorousness of the word 'Pallas' itself."

He concludes by saying:

"The undercurrent of meaning is rendered first apparent in the lines:

> Take thy beak from out my heart, and take thy form from off my door!
> Quoth the Raven, "Nevermore."

"It will be observed that the words 'from out my heart' involve the first metaphorical expression in the poem. They, with the answer, 'Nevermore,' dispose the mind to seek a moral in all that has been previously narrated. The reader begins now to regard the raven as emblematical—but it is not until the very last stanza that the intention of making him emblematical of *Mournful* and *Never-ending Remembrance* is permitted distinctly to be seen."

The mood of the poem is, therefore, hopeless despair, personified by the raven, over the loss of a loved one (real or imaginary) represented by the name Lenore. Accepting this as the true significance of the piece, lines which cannot be explained by any other interpretation are easily understood—such, for example, as "whom the angels name Lenore, nameless here forevermore"; "other friends have flown before"; "she shall press, ah, nevermore"; "thy memories of Lenore"; and all of the last two stanzas.

Poe may or may not have built the poem up in the method which he details at length in his *Philosophy of Composition,* but he certainly knew what he meant in writing it.

THE RAVEN

1

Once upon a midnight dreary, while I pondered, weak and weary,
Over many a quaint and curious volume of forgotten lore,
While I nodded, nearly napping, suddenly there came a tapping,
As of some one gently rapping, rapping at my chamber door.
" 'T is some visitor," I muttered, "tapping at my chamber door—
    Only this, and nothing more."

2

Ah, distinctly I remember, it was in the bleak December,
And each separate dying ember wrought its ghost upon the floor.
Eagerly I wished the morrow; vainly I had tried to borrow

From my books surcease of sorrow—sorrow for the lost
 Lenore—
For the rare and radiant maiden whom the angels name
 Lenore—
    Nameless here forevermore.

3

And the silken sad uncertain rustling of each purple
 curtain
Thrilled me—filled me with fantastic terrors never felt
 before;
So that now, to still the beating of my heart, I stood
 repeating,
" 'T is some visitor entreating entrance at my chamber
 door—
Some late visitor entreating entrance at my chamber
 door;—
    This it is and nothing more."

4

Presently my soul grew stronger; hesitating then no
 longer,
"Sir," said I, "or Madam, truly your forgiveness I
 implore;
But the fact is I was napping, and so gently you came
 rapping,
And so faintly you came tapping, tapping at my chamber
 door,

That I scarce was sure I heard you"—here I opened wide the door:—
    Darkness there, and nothing more.

5

Deep into that darkness peering, long I stood there wondering, fearing,
Doubting, dreaming dreams no mortal ever dared to dream before;
But the silence was unbroken, and the darkness gave no token,
And the only word there spoken was the whispered word, "Lenore!"
This I whispered, and an echo murmured back the word "Lenore!"
    Merely this and nothing more.

6

Back into the chamber turning, all my soul within me burning,
Soon again I heard a tapping, somewhat louder than before.
"Surely," said I, "surely that is something at my window lattice;
Let me see, then, what thereat is, and this mystery explore—
Let my heart be still a moment and this mystery explore;—
    'T is the wind and nothing more!"

7

Open then I flung the shutter, when, with many a flirt and flutter,
In there stepped a stately Raven of the saintly days of yore.
Not the least obeisance made he; not an instant stopped or stayed he;
But, with mien of lord or lady, perched above my chamber door—
Perched upon a bust of Pallas just above my chamber door—
    Perched, and sat, and nothing more.

8

Then this ebony bird beguiling my sad fancy into smiling,
By the grave and stern decorum of the countenance it wore,
"Though thy crest be shorn and shaven, thou," I said, "art sure no craven,
Ghastly, grim, and ancient Raven, wandering from the Nightly shore—
Tell me what thy lordly name is on the Night's Plutonian shore!"
    Quoth the Raven, "Nevermore."

9

Much I marvelled this ungainly fowl to hear discourse so plainly,

Though its answer little meaning—little relevancy bore;
For we cannot help agreeing that no living human being
Ever yet was blessed with seeing bird above his chamber door—
Bird or beast upon the sculptured bust above his chamber door
      With such name as "Nevermore."

10

But the Raven, sitting lonely on the placid bust, spoke only
That one word, as if his soul in that one word he did outpour.
Nothing further then he uttered; not a feather then he fluttered—
Till I scarcely more than muttered, "Other friends have flown before—
On the morrow *he* will leave me, as my Hopes have flown before."
      Then the bird said, "Nevermore."

11

Startled at the stillness broken by reply so aptly spoken,
"Doubtless," said I, "what it utters is its only stock and store,
Caught from some unhappy master, whom unmerciful Disaster

Followed fast and followed faster till his songs one burden bore—
Till the dirges of his Hope the melancholy burden bore
Of 'Never—nevermore.' "

12

But the Raven still beguiling all my sad soul into smiling,
Straight I wheeled a cushioned seat in front of bird and bust and door;
Then, upon the velvet sinking, I betook myself to linking
Fancy unto fancy, thinking what this ominous bird of yore—
What this grim, ungainly, ghastly, gaunt, and ominous bird of yore
    Meant in croaking "Nevermore."

13

This I sat engaged in guessing, but no syllable expressing
To the fowl whose fiery eyes now burned into my bosom's core;
This and more I sat divining, with my head at ease reclining
On the cushion's velvet lining that the lamp-light gloated o'er,

But whose velvet violet lining with the lamp-light gloating o'er,
>   *She* shall press, ah, nevermore!

14

Then, methought, the air grew denser, perfumed from an unseen censer,
Swung by seraphim whose foot-falls tinkled on the tufted floor.
"Wretch," I cried, "thy God hath lent thee,—by these angels he hath sent thee
Respite—respite and nepenthe from thy memories of Lenore!
Quaff, O, quaff this kind nepenthe, and forget this lost Lenore!"
>   Quoth the Raven, "Nevermore."

15

"Prophet!" said I, "thing of evil!—prophet still, if bird or devil!—
Whether Tempter sent, or whether tempest tossed thee here ashore,
Desolate yet all undaunted, on this desert land enchanted—
On this home by Horror haunted—tell me truly, I implore—
Is there—*is* there balm in Gilead?—tell me—tell me, I implore!"
>   Quoth the Raven, "Nevermore."

18

"Prophet!" said I, "thing of evil—prophet still, if bird or devil!—
By that Heaven that bends above us—by that God we both adore—
Tell this soul with sorrow laden, if, within the distant Aidenn,
It shall clasp a sainted maiden whom the angels name Lenore—
Clasp a rare and radiant maiden whom the angels name Lenore?"
    Quoth the Raven, "Nevermore."

17

"Be that word our sign of parting, bird or fiend!" I shrieked, upstarting—
"Get thee back into the tempest, and the Night's Plutonian shore!
Leave no black plume as a token of that lie thy soul hath spoken!
Leave my loneliness unbroken!—quit the bust above my door!
Take thy beak from out my heart, and take thy form from off my door!
    Quoth the Raven, "Nevermore."

16

And the Raven, never flitting, still is sitting, still is sitting

On the pallid bust of Pallas just above my chamber
    door;
And his eyes have all the seeming of a Demon's that is
    dreaming,
And the lamp-light o'er him streaming throws his
    shadow on the floor;
And my soul from out that shadow that lies floating on
    the floor
        Shall be lifted—*nevermore*.

                          —Edgar Allan Poe.

Pallas—the Athenian goddess of wisdom.
Plutonian—from Pluto, the mythological god of the lower regions.
Aidenn—Eden.
Respite—an interval of rest.
Nepenthe—a drug used by the ancients to give relief from pain and sorrow. Here it means forgetfulness.
Balm in Gilead—means cure—healing for his sorrow for his lost one. The reference is to *Jeremiah 8:22:* "Is there no balm in Gilead? is there no physician there?"

ARMAGEDDON

Here is a poem of courage, manliness, and the highest ideals; it is a noble battle-cry for the future of the human race. But these qualities are revealed to us only when we understand the historic significance of the name *Armageddon*. Without this knowledge "Marching down to Armageddon" is but an empty line.

Armageddon was another name for the hill or city of Megiddo, in the great plain of Esdraelon, which extends across central Palestine from the Mediterranean to the Jordan. It was the great battlefield of Old Testament history, the scene of many mighty struggles of good and evil—the old battlefield of Canaan. It was the scene of two great victories—those of Barak and Deborah over the Canaanites commanded by Sisera, and of Gideon over the Midianites—and of two great disasters—the death of Saul and the death of Jonathan.

> "The kings came and fought; then fought the kings of Caanan in Taanoch by the waters of Megiddo; they took no gain of money. They fought from heaven; the stars in their courses fought against Sisera."
>
> From the *Song of Deborah*.

> "For there the shield of the mighty ones was cast away,
> The shield of Saul, as of one unanointed with oil.
> From the blood of the slain, from the fat of the mighty
> The bow of Jonathan turned not back,
> And the sword of Saul returned not empty.
> Saul and Jonathan were lovely and pleasant in their lives,
> And in their death they were not divided."
>
> From *David's Lament*.

On the same historic plain near the city of Megiddo, Josiah, king of Judah, was defeated and mortally wounded by Necho, the Pharaoh of Egypt, 609 B. C.

The plain of Megiddo was so often, in fact, the meeting place of ancient armies that it seems to have come to be looked upon as the typical battleground.

In *Revelation* the evil spirits are spoken of as being gathered together "to the battle of that great day of God Almighty . . . into a place called in the Hebrew tongue Armageddon."

In this poem of Sir Edwin Arnold's, Armageddon with its historic significance is lifted out of the dim past and projected into the future; and "Marching down to Armageddon" means marching down to humanity's great battlefield of the future, where the forces of right and wrong are to contend, as of old, for supremacy.

As soldiers in the army marching on to this conflict our banner is the white banner of Hope, our motto, *Brotherhood;* a song is on our lips, and our bugle rings for the peace of the world. We have no hate for those who do not agree with us, and we complain not that the way we tread is so rough and long. This is the battle-cry of the future.

ARMAGEDDON

1

Marching down to Armageddon—
  Brothers, stout and strong!
Let us cheer the way we tread on,
  With a soldier's song!
Faint we by the weary road,
  Or fall we in the rout,
Dirge or Pæan, Death or Triumph!—
  Let the song ring out!

2

We are they who scorn the scorners—
  Love the lovers—hate
None within the world's four corners—
  All must share one fate;
We are they whose common banner
  Bears no badge nor sign,
Save the light which dyes it white—
  The Hope that makes it shine.

3

We are they whose bugle rings,
  That all the wars may cease;
We are they will pay the Kings
  Their cruel price for Peace;
We are they whose steadfast watchword
  Is what Christ did teach—
"Each man for his Brother first—
  And Heaven, then, for each."

4

We are they who will not falter—
  Many swords or few—
Till we make this Earth the altar
  Of a worship new;
We are they who will not take
  From palace, priest or code,
A meaner Law than "Brotherhood"—
  A lower Lord than God.

5

Marching down to Armageddon—
    Brothers, stout and strong!
Ask not why the way we tread on
    Is so rough and long!
God will tell us when our spirits
    Grow to grasp His plan!
Let us do our part to-day—
    And help Him, helping Man!

6

Shall we even curse the madness
    Which for "ends of State"
Dooms us to the long, long sadness
    Of this human hate?
Let us slay in perfect pity
    Those that must not live;
Vanquish, and forgive our foes—
    Or fall—and still forgive!

7

We are those whose unpaid legions,
    In free ranks arrayed,
Massacred in many regions—
    Never once were stayed:
We are they whose torn battalions,
    Trained to bleed, not fly,
Make our agonies a triumph,—
    Conquer, while we die!

8

Therefore, down to Armageddon—
　Brothers, bold and strong;
Cheer the glorious way we tread on,
　With this soldier song!
Let the armies of the old Flags
　March in silent dread!
Death and Life are one to us,
　Who fight for Quick and Dead!

　　　　　　　　—Edwin Arnold.

EACH AND ALL

This is one of Emerson's noblest poems; and although it seems to be difficult, it is not. High-school pupils can understand it, and teachers will find in it one of the greatest of all truths of nature and of life. It is worthy of much rereading and careful study.

The brackets and italics which we have had the printer use will assist in its interpretation. The central thought —the key-note—of the whole poem is expressed in the italicized lines:

　　All are needed by each one;
　　Nothing is fair or good alone.

This central thought is illustrated in seven different ways (each indicated by a bracket), and each of these illustrations should be studied closely in the light of the central thought of the poem.

After giving these seven illustrations of the truth he wants to teach, Emerson says:

Beauty is unripe childhood's cheat.

That is, beauty taken away from its natural environment or setting is not truth. In another poem, *The Rhodora* (page 159), he says that "beauty is its own excuse for being"—beauty when true to nature.

After this bit of philosophizing, he closes the poem with an illustration of each and all in proper harmony (last bracket), and yields himself to the influence of "the perfect whole."

Throughout the poem, from the first line to the last, may be found the great lesson of the power of influence. Perhaps it is most definitely expressed in the oft-quoted lines:

Nor knowest thou what argument
Thy life to thy neighbor's creed has lent.

This is a lesson which runs through all nature and all human life, and in no piece of literature has it been more beautifully or more effectively expressed than in *Each and All.*

EACH AND ALL

1 { Little thinks, in the field, yon red-cloaked clown,
    Of thee from the hill-top looking down;

2 { The heifer that lows in the upland farm,
    Far-heard, lows not thine ear to charm;

EACH AND ALL

3. The sexton, tolling his bell at noon,
Deems not that great Napoleon
Stops his horse and lists with delight
Whilst his files sweep round yon Alpine height;

4. Nor knowest thou what argument
Thy life to thy neighbor's creed has lent.

All are needed by each one;
Nothing is fair or good alone.

5. I thought the sparrow's note from heaven,
Singing at dawn on the alder bough;
I brought him home, in his nest, at even;
He sings the song, but it cheers not now;
For I did not bring home the river and the sky;
He sang to my ear,—they sang to my eye.

6. The delicate shells lay on the shore;
The bubbles of the latest wave
Fresh pearls to their enamel gave;
And the bellowing of the savage sea
Greeted their safe escape to me.
I wiped away the weeds and foam,
I fetched my sea-born treasures home;
But the poor, unsightly, noisome things
Had left their beauty on the shore,
With the sun and the sand and the wild uproar.

> 7. {
> The lover watched his graceful maid,
> As 'mid the virgin train she strayed,
> Nor knew her beauty's best attire
> Was woven still by the snow-white choir.
> At last she came to his hermitage,
> Like the bird from the woodlands to the cage;
> The gay enchantment was undone,—
> A gentle wife, but fairy none.
> }
>
> Then I said, "I covet truth;
> Beauty is unripe childhood's cheat;
> I leave it behind with the games of youth."
>
> 8. {
> As I spoke, beneath my feet
> The ground-pine curled its pretty wreath,
> Running over the club-moss burs;
> I inhaled the violet's breath;
> Around me stood the oaks and firs;
> Pine cones and acorns lay on the ground;
> Over me soared the eternal sky;
> Full of light and of deity;
> Again I saw, again I heard,
> The rolling river, the morning bird;
> Beauty through my senses stole;
> I yielded myself to the perfect whole.
> }
> —Ralph Waldo Emerson.

FATE

The mysterious decrees of Fate or of Providence are set forth in these verses. A few facts are given without comment. There was a storm at sea, and the intended passenger, acting wisely as he thought, did not sail. The woods were dangerous with wild beasts, and the hunter, acting wisely as he thought, did not join in the chase. The ship made the trip safely, and the hunters came home in glee; but meanwhile the town, which seemed to be perfectly safe, being builded upon a rock, was destroyed by an earthquake.

There are thousands of such incidents—a man goes safely through a dozen battles and is finally killed by the scratch of a pin. But there is no such thing as chance or luck or fate in the world. There is a cause for everything. The universe is governed by law, or through law, and law is not freakish.

FATE

1

"The sky is clouded, the rocks are bare;
The spray of the tempest is white in air;
The winds are out with the waves at play,
And I shall not tempt the sea to-day.

2

"The trail is narrow, the wood is dim,
The panther clings to the arching limb;
And the lion's whelps are abroad at play,
And I shall not join in the chase to-day."

By permission of Houghton Mifflin Company.

3

But the ship sailed safely over the sea,
And the hunters came from the chase in glee;
And the town that was builded upon a rock
Was swallowed up in the earthquake shock.

—Bret Harte.

FORTUNE

Enid's Song.

"Man is man and master of his fate," is the key-note of these lines. The proud may be affected by the turn of Fortune's wheel, but those whose hearts are great are the lords of their own hands and smile whether Fortune favors or whether she frowns. The staring crowd looks with wonder, but we are indifferent to ("we neither love nor hate") what is called Fortune, knowing that it is only a shadow in the clouds. Man is master of his fate.

FORTUNE

1

Turn, Fortune, turn thy wheel and lower the proud;
Turn thy wild wheel through sunshine, storm, and
 cloud;
 Thy wheel and thee we neither love nor hate.

2

Turn, Fortune, turn thy wheel with smile or frown;
With that wild wheel we go not up or down;
  Our hoard is little, but our hearts are great.

3

Smile and we smile, the lords of many lands;
Frown and we smile, the lords of our own hands;
  For man is man and master of his fate.

4

Turn, turn thy wheel above the staring crowd;
Thy wheel and thou are shadows in the cloud;
  Thy wheel and thee we neither love nor hate.
                                —Alfred Tennyson.

ULALUME

Ulalume is the saddest poem in American literature. It is wonderfully imaginative, beautiful, and musical, but to most readers it has no definite meaning. Its theme is the theme of nearly all of Poe's poems, especially of *The Raven* and *Annabel Lee*—grief for a lost loved one. In *Ulalume* it is grief for his young wife. Stated very imperfectly in prose, the meaning is this:

Ulalume, as he calls his wife, has been dead a year. This is the first anniversary of her burial, but he has, for the time being, forgotten the fact. Meanwhile some hint or thought of a new love is coming into his mind or heart. In the agony of his grief he is in deep communion with himself—with his subconscious self, with *"Psyche, his Soul."* Thought of the new affection presents itself and he is inclined to sanction it, for it seems to point to peace. But something (that something being *Psyche,* or his subconscious self) warns him against it. He tries to hush the voice of warning, and succeeds in pacifying its scruples. Suddenly he remembers that exactly a year ago he buried Ulalume. In agony and horror, he banishes the thought of the new love and cries out that some demon has been tempting him. It is like coming unexpectedly upon the grave of his wife when he had been thinking of someone else.

This tragedy of the soul is told figuratively and imaginatively, of course, and herein lies its great beauty; but it is none the less a powerful poem and an awful tragedy.

ULALUME

1

The skies they were ashen and sober;
   The leaves they were crispèd and sere,—
   The leaves they were withering and sere,—
It was night in the lonesome October
   Of my most immemorial year;
It was hard by the dim lake of Auber,
   In the misty mid-region of Weir,—
It was down by the dank tarn of Auber,
   In the ghoul-haunted woodland of Weir.

2

Here once, through an alley Titanic,
   Of cypress, I roamed with my soul,—
   Of cypress, with Psyche, my Soul.
These were days when my heart was volcanic
   As the scoriac rivers that roll—
   As the lavas that restlessly roll—
Their sulphurous currents down Yaanek
   In the ultimate climes of the pole—
That groan as they roll down Mount Yaanek,
   In the realms of the boreal pole.

3

Our talk had been serious and sober,
   But our thoughts they were palsied and sere,
   Our memories were treacherous and sere,—
For we knew not the month was October,
   And we marked not the night of the year,—
   (Ah, the night of all nights in the year!)
We noted not the dim lake of Auber—
   (Though once we had journeyed down here)—
Remembered not the dank tarn of Auber,
   Nor the ghoul-haunted woodland of Weir.

4

And now, as the night was senescent,
   And the star-dials pointed to morn,—
   As the star-dials hinted of morn,—

At the end of our path a liquescent
  And nebulous lustre was born,
Out of which a miraculous crescent
  Arose with a duplicate horn,—
Astarte's bediamonded crescent,
  Distinct with its duplicate horn.

5

And I said, "She is warmer than Dian:
  She rolls through an ether of sighs,—
  She revels in a region of sighs:
She has seen that the tears are not dry on
  These cheeks, where the worm never dies,
And has come past the stars of the Lion
  To point us the path to the skies,—
  To point us the path to the skies—
Come up, in despite of the Lion,
  To shine on us with her bright eyes,
Come up through the lair of the Lion,
  With love in her luminous eyes."

6

But Psyche, uplifting her finger,
  Said, "Sadly this star I mistrust,—
  Her pallor I strangely mistrust:
O hasten! O let us not linger!
  O fly!—let us fly!—for we must."
In terror she spoke, letting sink her
  Wings until they trailed in the dust,—

In agony sobbed, letting sink her
    Plumes till they trailed in the dust,—
    Till they sorrowfully trailed in the dust.

7

I replied, "This is nothing but dreaming:
    Let us on by this tremulous light!
    Let us bathe in this crystalline light!
Its sybilic splendor is beaming
    With Hope and in Beauty to-night:
    See! it flickers up the sky through the night!
Ah, we safely may trust to its gleaming,
    And be sure it will lead us aright.
We safely may trust to a gleaming
    That cannot but guide us aright,
    Since it flickers up to Heaven through the night."

8

Thus I pacified Psyche, and kissed her,
    And tempted her out of her gloom,—
    And conquered her scruples and gloom;
And we passed to the end of the vista,
    But were stopped by the door of a tomb,—
    By the door of a legended tomb:
And I said, "What is written, sweet sister,
    On the door of this legended tomb?"
    She replied, "Ulalume!—Ulalume!—
    'T is the vault of thy lost Ulalume!"

9

Then my heart it grew ashen and sober
    As the leaves that were crispèd and sere,—
    As the leaves that were withering and sere:
And I cried, "It was surely October,—
    On *this* very night of last year,
    That I journeyed—I journeyed down here,—
    On this night, of all nights in the year,
    Ah, what demon has tempted me here?
Well I know, now, this dim lake of Auber,—
    This misty mid-region of Weir,—
Well I know, now, this dank tarn of Auber,—
    This ghoul-haunted woodland of Weir."

—Edgar Allan Poe.

The first three stanzas portray the state of his mind—his heart is like the eruption of a volcano, and everything is as gloomy as a ghoul-haunted cypress woodland when the skies are ashen and gray. The names are invented—Auber, Weir, Yaanek—and their very sound harmonizes with the scene.

Astarte—another name for Venus, the goddess of love. This star with its nebulous lustre represents the faint new love against which his inner voice is protesting.

Immemorial—unforgetable.

Tarn—a little lake.

Senescent—growing old.

Arose with a duplicate horn—doubtless referring to its newness, to indicate the new love. It is the *new* moon and not the full moon which is in the form of a crescent with two horns.

Stars of the Lion—a constellation of stars called Leo or The Lion.

ULALUME

Dian—Diana (the goddess of the hunt) who scorned love.
Lethean—causing forgetfulness.

Sybilic—prophetic.

Stopped by the door of a tomb—suddenly remembered the anniversary of Ulalume's burial. It recalled him to his former state of mind, and with intensified grief he is plunged once more into the "ghoul-haunted woodland" of his soul.

It should be said that an entirely different interpretation of *Ulalume* is made by some critics. At the editor's request, *Dr. Edward Everett Hale, Jr.*, Professor of English in Union College, Schenectady, N. Y., has kindly given the meaning of the poem as he interprets it. Dr. Hale says:

"Who was this lost love mourned in so many poems? Those who believe it to have been some living, breathing woman (or women) create the curious condition of a man at once mourning the dead and devoted to the living, for Virginia Poe (who has been thought to be the object of *Annabel Lee*) was still living at the time of *The Raven*. Could Poe have suffered bitter regret for one love when he was absolutely happy with another? Certainly Poe needed no real woman to mourn; there were other things he might have mourned if he had chosen, under the type of a beautiful woman. He might have mourned his lost ideal of classic beauty. He was a romanticist, and his ideal of classic beauty was utterly lost to him forever. Poe looked back upon classic beauty and realized that he could never again possess it in the perfect form in which he had known it once. That, I take it, was at the bottom of the mood which created his greater poems, and particularly *Ulalume*. The poet has had his ideal of beauty and it is gone, and is buried by himself in a fantastic region of romance. But because that ideal is gone forever, his mind does not cease to act. He still wanders with Psyche his soul. And in one wandering he fancies that he has found something that will lead him once more to that peace with beauty that he knew. In spite of the warning of Psyche he follows until he suddenly realizes that he is but going on a path he has trodden before, he will but end at the door which keeps him ever separate from his ideal.

"Let it not seem absurd that we should imagine a man to grieve over the loss of an ideal of beauty as keenly as we might grieve over the loss of some beautiful love. When a poet cares as much for ideals as Poe did, and so little for real people, the wonder is that any one should have ever thought otherwise."

PROSPICE

Prospice means *look forward*. The poem is a defiance of death, the "Arch Fear." It would be hard to find anything more intensely dramatic or anything nobler on the subject. He approaches "the post of the foe"— Death—with eyes unbandaged and with a heroism truly sublime. It is the supreme test of the spirit's mastery, and the spirit stands the test like a strong man, and gains "the reward of it all." He estimates death at its fullest import, when "the worst turns the best to the brave."

The poem was written a short time after Mrs. Browning's death—a fact which explains the closing lines and adds beauty and pathos to them.

Every line is crowded with meaning and should be studied closely. As here interpreted, death is "the climax and fruition of life."

PROSPICE

PROSPICE

Fear death?—to feel the fog in my throat,
  The mist in my face,
When the snows begin, and the blasts denote
  I am nearing the place,
The power of the night, the press of the storm,
  The post of the foe;
Where he stands, the Arch Fear in a visible form,
  Yet the strong man must go;
For the journey is done and the summit attained
  And the barriers fall,
Though a battle's to fight ere the guerdon be gained,
  The reward of it all.
I was ever a fighter, so—one fight more,
  The best and the last!
I would hate that death bandaged my eyes, and forbore,
  And bade me creep past.
No! let me taste the whole of it, fare like my peers,
  The heroes of old,
Bear the brunt, in a minute pay glad life's arrears
  Of pain, darkness and cold.
For sudden the worse turns the best to the brave,
  The black minute's at end,
And the elements' rage, the fiend-voices that rave,
  Shall dwindle, shall blend,
Shall change, shall become first a peace out of pain,
  Then a light, then thy breast,

O thou soul of my soul! I shall clasp thee again,
    And with God be the rest!

—Robert Browning.

CROSSING THE BAR

Of this poem Tennyson's son says:

"It was written in my father's eighty-first year, on a day in October when we came from Aldworth to Farringford. Before reaching Farringford he had the 'moaning of the bar' in his mind, and after dinner he showed me this poem written out. I said, 'This is the crown of your life's work.' He answered, 'It came in a moment.' He explained the 'Pilot' as 'That Divine and Unseen who is always guiding us.' A few days before my father's death he said to me: 'Mind you put *Crossing the Bar* at the end of all editions of my poems.'"

Farringford is on the Isle of Wight, where Tennyson lived, and the strait between the mainland and the island is the one they were crossing when the poem came to Tennyson's mind.

Crossing the Bar is a good example of the imaginative treatment of a few familiar facts of nature and life, converting them thereby into a great piece of art. The materials of the poem are the sunset, the twilight, the evening bell and the evening star, the tide moaning on the sandy bar and the tide full and calm and deep, the uncertain dark, the welcome call from the farther shore, and then the glorified face of the Master and Pilot. Not a word is said about old age, not a word about death; it is all treated imaginatively. And what is the result? Three noble emotions are aroused—*first*, beauty; for any genuine poem or any genuine piece of art whatever will arouse the emotion of beauty; *second*, pleasure; for beauty wherever seen and felt gives pleasure; and, *third*, trust. This last is here the predominant emotion.

CROSSING THE BAR

1

Sunset and evening star,
    And one clear call for me:
And may there be no moaning of the bar,
    When I put out to sea.

2

But such a tide as moving seems asleep,
    Too full for sound and foam,
When that which drew from out the boundless deep
    Turns again home.

3

Twilight and evening bell,
    And after that the dark:
And may there be no sadness of farewell,
    When I embark.

4

> For tho' from out our bourne of Time and Place
>   The flood may bear me far,
> I hope to see my Pilot face to face
>   When I have crost the bar.

—Alfred Tennyson.

When that which drew from out the boundless deep—means, of course, the soul, the individual personality.

Bourne—a boundary, a limit.

Compare with this poem the lines of Whittier:

> And so beside the Silent Sea
>   I wait the muffled oar;
> No harm from Him can come to me
>   On ocean or on shore.
>
> I know not where His islands lift
>   Their fronded palms in air;
> I only know I cannot drift
>   Beyond His love and care.

Landor's calm and stoical farewell:

> I warmed both hands before the fire of life,
> It sinks and I am ready to depart.

Emerson's *Terminus:*

> As the bird trims her to the gale,
>   I trim myself to the storm of time,
> I man the rudder, reef the sail,
>   Obey the voice at eve obeyed at prime:
> Lowly faithful, banish fear,
>   Right onward drive unharmed;
> The port, well worth the cruise, is near,
>   And every wave is charmed.

David, in the twenty-third *Psalm:*

Yea, though I walk through the valley of the shadow of death, I will fear no evil: for Thou *art* with me; Thy rod and Thy staff they comfort me.

And Longfellow, in *Resignation:*

> There is no Death! What seems so is transition;
> This life of mortal breath
> Is but a suburb of the life elysian,
> Whose portal we call death.

FINIS

BIOGRAPHICAL NOTES OF THE AUTHORS REPRESENTED

Alexander, Cecil Frances (Humphreys).—Born in Ireland in 1830, and married Rev. William Alexander, afterwards Bishop of Derry. She wrote many hymns for children, and poems on Old Testament subjects, the best of them being *The Burial of Moses*. She died October 12, 1895.

Arnold, Edwin (Sir).—Born January 10, 1832, in Sussex, England, and died in London, March 24, 1904. He was educated at University College, Oxford, became principal of the government Sanscrit College at Poonah, India, was editor of the London *Daily Telegraph*, and lived in Japan for some time. He was a student of the literature and life of the Eastern peoples and his poems deal with the Orient. *The Indian Song of Songs, Pearls of the Faith, The Light of Asia*, and *The Light of the World*, are the most widely known. *The Light of Asia* deals with Buddha, and *The Light of the World* with Christ.

Browning, Robert.—Born May 7, 1812, at Camberwell, England. He was educated privately, devoted himself wholly to literature, and died in 1889, in Italy, where he spent much of his life. His wife was Elizabeth Barrett Browning, also a distinguished poet. Browning's fame came slowly, his genius was much disputed by critics, and for a long time he was ignored by the public. His language is eccentric and sometimes obscure, but his thought is deep and subtle; and Browning and Tennyson stand side by side as the great poets of the latter part of the 19th century. His theme is always the human soul, generally studied under exceptional circumstances. *The Ring and the Book, Pippa Passes, My Last Duchess, Prospice, Saul, Rabbi Ben Ezra, The Laboratory, Childe Roland to the Dark Tower Came, Abt Vogler, The Bishop Orders His Tomb at St. Praxed's Church* are some of the great things written by him.

Bryant, William Cullen.—Born at Cummington, Massachusetts, 1794, and died in New York City, 1878. Famous both as a poet and as the editor of the New York *Evening Post,* being the chief editor of that journal for more than half a century. After two terms at Williams College he studied law and practiced this profession for nine years at Plainfield and Great Barrington, Massachusetts; but he found himself out of place and thereafter gave himself to poetry and journalism. He was the real founder of American poetry. *Thanatopsis* was published in 1817, and his first volume of poems in 1821. Notwithstanding the fact that he spent the greater part of his life in New York his poetry is the poetry of the New England landscape and life. Read *Thanatopsis, Lines to a Waterfowl, The Yellow Violet, The Fringed Gentian, The Forest Hymn, The Death of the Flowers, Autumn Woods, The Ages, Inscription for the Entrance to a Wood,* and *Green River.*

Burns, Robert.—Born January 25, 1759, in Ayrshire, Scotland, the son of a small farmer. The family was poor and the son received but little regular education; he was "a hardworked plowboy." But he was a great reader, having a book before him even at meal times. He early began writing songs of country life that attracted attention, and he was recognized and lionized, as a real genius. In 1789 he was appointed exciseman for the government. He died July 21, 1796, only thirty-seven years of age, having led a life mixed of misery, remorse, and happiness, his few peaceful years being those he lived as a farmer in Dumfrieshire with his wife, Jean Armour. Like Poe, although his life was miserable, his fame is immortal. His love songs are among the finest ever written. *The Cotter's Saturday Night, Tam O'Shanter, The Twa Dogs, To a Mountain Daisy, To a Mouse, To Mary in Heaven, Highland Mary, Ye Banks and Braes O' Bonnie Doon, Flow Gently, Sweet Afton, O, My Luve's Like a Red, Red Rose, Scots wha hae wi' Wallace Bled,* and *Is There for Honest Poverty* are the glory of Scotland's literature.

Byron, George Gordon (Lord).—Born in London, January 22, 1788, and died of a fever at Missolonghi, Greece, October 19, 1824, while aiding the Greeks to free themselves from Turkish despotism. By birth he was entitled to a seat in the English House of Lords, but he spent his life in travel and in writing. His first book of poems, *Hours of Idleness,* was ridiculed by critics, but he lived to see himself the most famous author in all Europe, although he died at thirty-six. His personality as much as his literary genius contributed to the spell which he threw over the world. Proud, passionate, handsome, fascinating, he captivated all who came within his reach. The story of his own exploits was as interesting to the public as anything he wrote. After his death his fame greatly diminished, but his place in the literary world is still a large one. *Childe Harold's Pilgrimage* and *Don Juan* are his greatest productions. His greatest dramas are *Manfred* and *Cain*. Among his shorter poems *The Prisoner of Chillon, The Destruction of Sennacherib, She Walks in Beauty, To Thomas Moore,* are representative.

Campbell, Thomas.—Born in Glasgow, Scotland, in 1777, educated at the University of Glasgow, resided at Edinburgh, London, and Boulogne, was three times Rector of the University of Glasgow, died in 1844, and was buried in Westminster Abbey. His famous war-odes are among the best war-poetry of England. *Hohenlinden, The Battle of the Baltic, Ye Mariners of England,* are full of martial music. Other poems of his are *Lord Ullin's Daughter, O'Connor's Child, The Spectre Boat.* His longer poems, *Gertrude of Wyoming, The Pleasures of Hope,* and *Theodoric* are no longer read.

Clough, Arthur Hugh.—Born at Liverpool, England, January 1, 1819, and died in 1861 at Florence. He studied at Rugby and Oxford, and spent some time in the United States during his childhood and later in life; became the head of University Hall, London, which he held for a short time, and later filled a position in the Education office. Clough was a poet of doubt, though not of despair. *Say Not the Struggle, Qua Cursum Ventus, Where Lies the Land,* and *The Shadow* are among his best poems.

Drake, Joseph Rodman.—Born in New York City, 1795, and died in 1820, of consumption. Although he lived to be only twenty-five years old he wrote *The Culprit Fay,* and *The American Flag,* both of which are still read. The late George Bancroft, the historian, considered *The Culprit Fay* the finest thing in American literature, but not many persons hold this opinion.

Eastman, Julia Arabella.—See *page* 237.

Emerson, Ralph Waldo.—Born May 25, 1803, in Boston, where he resided for thirty years, and died April 27, 1882, at Concord, where his home was the literary centre of America. He was graduated from Harvard in 1821, and some years later from the Harvard Divinity School. For a few years he engaged in the active ministry of the Congregational Church in Boston. The rest of his life was devoted to lecturing, writing and thinking, with three visits to Europe. He was our greatest seer and our most original thinker. Perhaps America has produced no finer mind than his. His writings are of two classes—essays and poems, for his lectures are really essays. Such poems as *The Problem, The Rhodora, The Concord Hymn, Each and All, Brahma, The Snow Storm, Good Bye, Wood Notes,* and *Terminus* are immortal. Among his greatest essays are *Nature, The American Scholar, Self-Reliance, Friendship, Compensation, History,* and *Character.* No other writer has so enriched American thought; no other writer has had such influence upon the best minds of the country.

Harte, Francis Bret.—Born in Albany, New York, in 1839 and died in London in 1902. He went to California when he was about sixteen and became by turns school teacher, miner, printer, newspaper writer, and editor. In 1868 he founded the *Overland Monthly* in San Francisco. He is best known as a writer of stories of life in California in the mining days. The best of these are *The Luck of Roaring Camp, The Outcasts of Poker Flat, Tennessee's Partner, Brown of Calaveras,* and *How Santa Claus Came to Simpson's Bar.* These tales are intensely dramatic, and full of humor, pathos, and power. His later years were spent in London.

Holmes, Oliver Wendell.—Born in Cambridge, Massachusetts, August 29, 1809, and died in Boston in 1894. He was educated at Harvard, graduating there in the famous class of 1829. For thirty-five years he was professor of anatomy and physiology in that institution. He was a poet, an essayist, a novelist, a man of science, a wit, a humorist, a teacher—and famous in everything he tried. His writings are the best representation in our literature of the cultured life of Boston. "He was the laureate of Harvard and of Boston." In poetry his best work is *The Chambered Nautilus, The Last Leaf, Old Ironsides, The One-Hoss Shay,* and *The Living Temple.* His informal essays are grouped in the Autocrat Series—*The Autocrat at the Breakfast Table, The Professor at the Breakfast Table, The Poet at the Breakfast Table,* and *Over the Teacups.* The latter was written when he was eighty years of age. His novels are *Elsie Venner, The Guardian Angel,* and *A Mortal Antipathy,* all dealing with the problem of heredity. Holmes was not a profound or original thinker, but he knew many sides of life remarkably well and he told what he knew with great grace and polish.

Hood, Thomas.—Born in London, May, 1799, and died in May, 1845. His best known poems are *The Bridge of Sighs,* and *The Song of the Shirt,* but he wrote many other

graceful and pathetic or humorous pieces. He devoted
much of his life to journalism.

Hunt, Leigh.—Born at Southgate, England, October
19, 1784, and died August 28, 1859. He was educated at
Oxford; was editor of *The Examiner;* was imprisoned for
libel on the Prince Regent; later received a pension from
the Crown. He spent some years in Italy. He wrote
much graceful and cheerful prose, and *The Story of Rimini,
Abou Ben Adhem, Nile, Jenny Kissed Me, The Grasshopper
and the Cricket,* and other fine things in verse.

Ingelow, Jean.—Born in 1830; died 1897. A popular
English poet and story-writer, best remembered by her
poem *High Tide on the Coast of Lincolnshire.*

Jackson, Helen Hunt.—Born at Amherst, Massachusetts, 1831 (daughter of Professor W. W. Fiske of Amherst College) and married Captain E. B. Hunt, an army
engineer. After his death she married W. S. Jackson of
Colorado Springs. Her greatest achievement was *Ramona,*
a romance of Indian life, a powerful plea for the rights of
the Indian. She died in 1885. *Resurgam, Down to Sleep,
Spinning, My Legacy, Joy,* and *Thought* are her best
poems. But she will be best remembered for her *Ramona*
and *A Century of Dishonor.*

Keats, John.—Born in London, October 29, 1795. Was
apprenticed for five years to a surgeon, but took to verse-
making and abandoned the profession of surgery. His
health was not robust and in 1820 he went to Italy. He
died there in 1821 of consumption and was buried in the
Protestant cemetery at Rome. Although he died at twenty-

five Matthew Arnold classes him with Shakespeare. Certainly so great a name in poetry was never made so young. There is nothing greater of their kind in English literature than the *Ode to a Nightingale, Ode on a Grecian Urn, To Autumn, On First Looking into Chapman's Homer, La Belle Dame sans Merci, The Eve of St. Agnes,* and *Lamia.*

Key, Francis Scott.—Born in Frederick county, Maryland, 1779, educated at St. Johns College, and practiced law in Washington, D. C. He died in 1843 and was buried at Frederick City, Maryland. His miscellaneous poems were collected and published after his death, but *The Star-Spangled Banner* is his only poem of importance.

Kingsley, Charles.—Born June 18, 1819, in Devonshire, England. He was educated at King's College, London, and at Cambridge University, and became Rector at Eversley in 1844, which position he held the remainder of his life—until January 23, 1875. Also for nine years he was Professor of modern history at Cambridge and later he was made Canon of Chester, Canon of Westminster, and Chaplain to the Queen. He is best known as a novelist from *Hypatia, Westward Ho, Alton Locke,* and *The Water Babies.* He wrote but little poetry, but all of it is pleasing, for example, *The Sands o' Dee, The Three Fishers,* and *When All the World is Young.*

Kipling, Rudyard.—Born at Bombay, India, of English parents, December 30, 1865, was educated at the United Service College, travelled in China, Japan, America, Africa, and Australia; lived for some time in the United States after marrying Miss Carolen Starr Balestier, an American. His home is now in London, but he is really a citizen of the world. Mr. Kipling has published much in both prose and verse, and is the most widely read of living English writers. Among his books are *Plain Tales from the Hills, Barrackroom Ballads, The Jungle Books, Many Inventions, The Seven Seas, Captains Courageous, The Day's Work, Kim,* etc.

Longfellow, Henry Wadsworth.—Born at Portland, Maine, February 27, 1807, was graduated from Bowdoin College in 1825, studied for the next three years in France, Spain, Italy, and Germany, taught modern languages for five years at Bowdoin, again studied two years abroad, and then began his work as professor of modern languages at Harvard, which he continued until 1854. From that date until his death, in Cambridge, in 1882, he devoted himself to literary work. While abroad and during his career as a college professor he wrote much in both verse and prose. He is the most widely read of American poets, standing supreme as the poet of the heart and the home. He added beauty, grace, sentiment and European culture to American poetry. *Evangeline, Hiawatha, The Courtship of Miles Standish, The Rainy Day, The Skeleton in Armor, Excelsior, The Village Blacksmith, The Psalm of Life, The Old Clock on the Stairs, The Arrow and the Song, The Day Is Done, Paul Revere's Ride, The Building of the Ship, The Bridge* and *The Wreck of the Hesperus,* are some of his poems that are familiar everywhere.

Lowell, James Russell.—Born in Cambridge, Massachusetts, February 22, 1819, in the old mansion at Elmwood, where he passed his life and where he died in 1891. He was graduated from Harvard in 1838. In 1840 he was admitted to the bar, but never practiced, for he at once devoted himself to literature. For twenty years, beginning in 1857, he was professor of modern languages at Harvard, succeeding Longfellow. Like Longfellow he had prepared himself by studying abroad. He was one of the founders, and for the first five years editor, of the *Atlantic Monthly*, and later was one of the editors of the *North American Review*. In 1877 he was appointed Minister to Spain, and in 1880 transferred to London. Lowell was our greatest literary critic, one of our greatest scholars, and in some respects our greatest poet. At his death in 1891 he was generally considered the foremost citizen of the country. *The Vision of Sir Launfal, The Biglow Papers, A Fable for Critics, The Commemoration Ode, Under the Willows, The First Snow Fall, An Indian Summer Reverie, Under the Old Elm, Rhoecus* and *The Cathedral* represent his best poetry. His *Essays in Criticism* are the high water mark of American criticism.

Luders, Charles Henry.—Born in Philadelphia, 1858, and died there in 1891. He wrote *The Dead Nymph and Other Poems* and *Hallo, My Fancy*. He was a poet of imagination and considerable power.

Montgomery, James.—Born in Ayrshire, Scotland, 1771, and died 1854. For more than thirty years he was the editor of *The Sheffield Iris,* a weekly paper. Twice he was imprisoned for publishing seditious articles. Among his poems are *Greenland, The Wanderer in Switzerland, The West Indies* and *Make Way for Liberty*. In 1833 he was granted a pension of three hundred pounds.

Mackay, Charles.—Born 1814, died 1889. An English journalist, who wrote a good deal of both verse and prose, the latter including *Tubal Cain, A Good Time Coming* and *O Ye Tears.*

Miller, Joaquin (his real name is Cincinnatus Hiner Miller).—Born in Indiana in 1841, has lived in Oregon, Nicaragua, Washington, London and California. While in Nicaragua he joined a tribe of Indians and became their sachem. Since 1887 he has resided in California. He has written both prose and poetry of a picturesque and stirring quality. *Songs of the Sierras, The Ship of the Desert, The Danites* and *Shadows of Shasta* are typical. His best short poem is perhaps *Columbus.*

Moore, Thomas.—Born in Dublin, May 28, 1779, resided in London, where he was a great social favorite, traveled in the United States and Canada, and died February 25, 1852. During his life he was immensely popular, and was considered a great poet, but to-day his rank is not so high. *Lalla Rookh, Irish Melodies* and *The Loves of the Angels* used to be read by everybody.

Piatt, Sarah Morgan Bryan.—Born in Kentucky in 1836, but has spent much of her life in Ohio. She has written many poems for children, besides *The New World and Other Poems, A Voyage to the Fortunate Isles, In Primrose Time,* etc.

Poe, Edgar Allan.—Born in Boston, January 19, 1809, the son of members of the theatrical profession, was adopted upon their death by John Allan of Richmond, studied for one session at the University of Virginia, later, after enlisting in the regular army and serving for two years, was appointed to West Point, but after ten months there was expelled. The rest of his life was spent in literary and journalistic work in Baltimore, New York, Philadelphia and Richmond. Most of the time he was in poverty and distress. He died in Baltimore, October 7, 1849. The story of his life is a sad and tragic one. Poe's great fame rests upon a half dozen short poems, and a few brief prose romances. *The Raven, Ulalume, The Bells, To Helen, The Haunted Palace, Israfel* and *Annabel Lee* are familiar everywhere. His best short stories are *The Fall of the House of Usher, Ligeia, The Gold Bug* and *The Murders in the Rue Morgue.* Poe stands as one of the three or four greatest names in American literature. "He was great in his genius, unhappy in his life, wretched in his death, but in his fame he is immortal."

Read, Thomas Buchanan.—Born 1822 and died in 1872. Most of his life was spent in Philadelphia, Cincinnati, Florence and Rome. He believed himself to be more of an artist than a poet, but his pictures are piled away in art store cellars, while *Sheridan's Ride, Drifting, The Closing Scene, The Wagoner of the Alleghanies* (especially the lyric beginning "The maid who binds her warrior's sash") are a genuine, if not weighty, contribution to American literature.

Shakespeare, William.—Born at Stratford-on-Avon, England, April 23, 1564, and died there April 23, 1616. He attended a school of academic grade. In 1582 he married Anne Hathaway, daughter of a neighboring farmer. In 1585 he went to London, where for twenty years he made his home, employed in some capacity at one of the playhouses, later as a member of the company, and in writing his immortal dramas. He played principal parts in his own dramas, which followed one another in rapid succession. He returned to Stratford-on-Avon about 1610 or 1612 in good circumstances. Shakespeare's name is the greatest in English letters. *Hamlet, Macbeth, Merchant of Venice, Julius Caesar, The Tempest, Twelfth Night* and *Lear* are a part of the thought of the English-speaking world. He was buried in the parish church at Stratford, and his tomb bears this inscription, written by himself:

> "Good friend for Jesus sake forbear
> To dig the dust enclosed here;
> Blest be the man that spares these stones
> And curst be he that moves my bones."

Southey, Robert.—Born at Bristol, England, August 12, 1774, educated at Oxford, and died near Keswick in 1843. In 1813 he was made Poet Laureate. His was a life of industrious authorship, after he had tried to study both medicine and law. His best prose work is the *Life of Nelson*, and in poetry he is best known by *The Curse of Kehama, Roderick* and *After Blenheim*.

Tennyson, Alfred (Lord).—Born August 6, 1809, at Somersby, England, educated at Trinity College, Cambridge, and devoted his whole life to poetry. His reputation grew steadily. In 1850 he became Poet Laureate. Three years later he took up his residence at Farringford in the Isle of Wight, which was his home the rest of his life. In 1883 he was raised to the Peerage. The story of his life is simple, but for more than half a century "he held the poetic supremacy almost unchallenged," and his name is one of the half dozen chief names in English poetry. He died October 6, 1892, and was buried with unequaled solemnity by the side of Chaucer in Westminster Abbey. He was the most representative poet of the last half of the 19th century. His greatest poems are *The Idylls of the King, In Memoriam, Locksley Hall, The Palace of Art, The Lotus-Eaters, The Brook, Sir Galahad, Break, Break, Break, Ulysses, The Vision of Sin* and *Crossing the Bar*.

Thaxter, Celia.—Born in the Isle of Shoals off the coast of New Hampshire in 1835, where she spent much of her life. Died in 1894. Her writings are full of the sounds and colors and odors of the northern sea. *Among the Isles of Shoals* is a charming prose study of the ocean. Her best poems are *The Sandpiper, Before Sunrise, The Watch of Boon Island* and *The Spaniards' Graves*.

Whitman, Walt.—Born at West Hills, Long Island, thirty miles from New York City, in 1819, and died at Camden, New Jersey, 1892. His school education was slight, and he worked as gardener, printer, and carpenter in many of the principal cities north and south. During the civil war he was an army nurse in Washington and in the south, tending the northern and southern wounded alike. He called himself the poet of democracy and many have taken him at his word. His best work is in such lyrics as *Out of the Cradle Endlessly Rocking, When Lilacs Last in the Dooryard Bloomed, Captain, My Captain,* and *The Man-of-War Bird*. They are among the treasures of our literature.

Whittier, John Greenleaf.—Born at Haverhill, Massachusetts, December 17, 1807, and died at Danvers, Massachusetts, September 7, 1892. He was country-born and country-bred, and his school education was meager, being obtained at the country school and at a neighboring academy where he spent a year. All of his life he was a Quaker. When he was twenty he took up journalism, and was engaged in Boston, Hartford, and Philadelphia. From 1840 until his death he lived at Amesbury or at Danvers, Massachusetts. He never married. In journalism as well as in poetry he was an earnest advocate of the anti-slavery cause. Whittier was our best poet of simple country life and nature. He was in an especial sense the poet of New England. His most characteristic poem is *Snow-Bound, a Winter Idyll*. Other poems most worthy of attention are *The Barefoot Boy, Telling the Bees, Among the Hills, Maud Muller, Ichabod, Laus Deo, The Pine Tree, Abraham Davenport, Cassandra Southwick, The Tent on the Beach, Corn Song,* and *The Eternal Goodness.*

Wolfe, Charles.—Born 1791, died 1823. An English clergyman whose only poem worth remembering is *The Burial of Sir John Moore.*

Eastman, Julia Arabella.—A Massachusetts teacher who has written a number of juvenile tales, among which are *Short Comings, Long Goings, Young Rich,* and *Kitty Kent's Troubles.* Born in New York in 1837. [*Adams's Dictionary of American Authors.*]